VIEW FROM THE CENTER

My Football Life
and the Rebirth
of Chiefs Kingdom

Tim Grunhard
with David Smale

TRIUMPH
BOOKS

Library of Congress Cataloging-in-Publication Data is available upon request.

This book is available in quantity at special discounts for your group or organization. For further information, contact:

Triumph Books LLC
814 North Franklin Street
Chicago, Illinois 60610
(312) 337-0747
www.triumphbooks.com

Printed in U.S.A.
ISBN: 978-1-63727-112-4
Design by NordCompo

To the Kansas City Chiefs Kingdom and its fans.
My play reflected your love and dedication
to the Chiefs organization.

Contents

Foreword *by Carl Peterson*. 7

Introduction 9

1   Emotion. 13

2   Born Hungry. 23

3   Notre Dame, Lou Holtz, and the NFL Draft 39

4   The Rebirth of a Kingdom 73

5   My Teammates 99

6   My Favorite Games. 141

7   The Impact of Marty Schottenheimer
    and Carl Peterson. 173

8   Paying It Back 203

Acknowledgments 231

Foreword

WHEN THE KANSAS CITY CHIEFS DECIDED TO DRAFT TIM GRUNHARD in the second round of the 1990 NFL Draft, we were looking for winners who could change the trajectory of the team. They had gone for so long with poor-performing teams. The franchise had a tradition of voting a new member into the Ring of Honor every year, and we needed players of that caliber. We believed if Tim could play to his abilities, he had a good chance to be an excellent player for the Chiefs and maybe someday be in that Ring of Honor.

More than success on the field, I knew we needed success off the field. The fanbase had become apathetic. With guys like Tim getting into the community and immersing themselves, the community was able to see these players and become fast friends with them. The first time you met Tim Grunhard, you liked him. You wanted to be around him and cheer for him. Tim was definitely one of the guys to fit the mold we were hoping for.

On the football side, when we scouted Tim, we saw a lot of excellent attributes, starting with the ability to play football. He was exceptional at it. The big concern was whether he could play center because he had been a guard at Notre Dame.

After assurances from his Notre Dame position coach, Marty Schottenheimer and I felt good about that.

The No. 1 thing I remember about Tim was his relentless tenacity. He had the heart of a lion, and you need that as an offensive lineman because you take a lot of punishment. But you've got a job to do, and Tim did it exceptionally well. Lou Holtz had only superlatives to say about Tim, his intelligence, and ability to adapt. Tim played in a lot of big games at Notre Dame, and the big stage did not seem to faze him.

The other thing we found in our research is that he was always an upbeat guy and a team guy. That's what you look for. You want to get guys who play football because they love the game. The guys you want to stay away from are the guys who are only interested in the money, and you can usually tell that right away. Tim certainly never gave us that impression.

Tim was interested in helping the people around him. After we drafted him, I told him that I needed him to stay in Kansas City in the offseason. I needed him to engage in the community. He readily accepted that and very quickly he became a fan favorite. He and his wife were involved in many benevolent activities and they continue to be.

This book does an excellent job of retelling those stories from the 1990s, not only the success we had on the field, but also off of it. Tim was such an integral part of what became known as Chiefs Kingdom. It was so fun to relive the glory days that I read this entire book in a day and a half, and I believe Tim does a great job of letting the reader know how it happened.

—*Carl Peterson*
Kansas City Chiefs President, General Manager, and CEO
1989–2008

Introduction

THE CAPTAIN SAID, "WE ARE MAKING OUR FINAL DESCENT INTO Kansas City."

As we were approaching from the south on my first flight to Kansas City after the 1990 NFL Draft, I looked out the window, and the city opened up to me. I just had this weird feeling that I was finding my new home. As we landed, I looked out the window, and there were cows in a field right by the runway.

I remember thinking it was kind of surreal. The last five minutes of that flight, which I've done hundreds of times since then, told me all I needed to know about Kansas City. It's a city with a lot of urban flair and a lot of great cultural entities and organizations, but it still has its roots in the prairies of Kansas and Missouri.

View from the Center talks about the people who live in this city and the team they root for and live and die for every Sunday. Whether they live in the urban center of Kansas City or on a ranch or a farm outside Kansas City, that one team, the Kansas City Chiefs, affects them all. I talk about the men, the games, and the struggles that built the foundation for what we now call

Chiefs Kingdom. This foundation, which was started in the 1960s, was rebuilt in the 1990s.

For the past 20 years, I've been on the radio sharing stories about my love and enthusiasm for the Chiefs and Chiefs fans. One of the reasons I do radio, and one of the reasons I think I'm good at it, is because I want to help people enjoy the game that I love so much. I decided to write this book so that people could see and understand the special decade of the 1990s, which changed the trajectory of the franchise. We had so many special men and special games that happened during that decade. I think it's fun to go behind the curtain and learn about those great characters who roamed the field and the hallways of the team headquarters in the '90s for the Chiefs.

I wanted to put those stories on paper so that the legacy of the Chiefs in the 1990s would never be forgotten. The idea started to percolate as the Chiefs exploded on the national scene. As Patrick Mahomes lifted up the Lombardi Trophy two weeks after Chiefs Hall of Famer Bobby Bell handed the Lamar Hunt Trophy to Clark Hunt, I knew I wanted to talk about the men and the games that helped rebuild the foundation.

All this came to fruition when I connected with David Smale. He has published about two dozen books, mostly on sports history. My dear friend and longtime Kansas City sportscaster, Frank Boal, introduced us. After looking at some of the books David had written, it really spiked my interest in telling this story. I've always been a student of history. I think we enjoy the present more by studying the past. That's why I love a lot of the books that David wrote. Just as those books are in-depth looks at history, I wanted to tell my own. I knew that David had the experience and the ability to help me formulate this story that I always wanted to tell.

Putting my experiences and my love for the Chiefs on paper helped me to remember all the great things that we accomplished. Teams are measured by Super Bowls and playoff wins, but I think that these teams should be measured by the dedication and the ability to rebuild and restart and to get the train rolling again.

I hope you enjoy this journey through my memory of the events of the 1990s with the Chiefs.

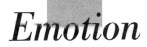

1

Emotion

I WALKED INTO ARROWHEAD STADIUM FOR A *MONDAY NIGHT Football* game on November 1, 2021, as I had done so many times in my 11-year career and in the more than two decades after that. But this night was different. Even driving into the stadium was kind of a surreal experience. Every time I drive up to One Arrowhead Drive, I consider it my second home because that's where my "family" lives. But this time it was kind of like a birthday party or wedding because the peripheral events of the evening, besides the game itself, were set up to honor me. I was really humbled by that.

I was inducted into the Kansas City Chiefs Ring of Honor and Hall of Fame.

It was like walking into a family reunion. That was one of the key things that I talked about in my speech and how I really feel. It is so special to be part of the Chiefs organization because it has been my family. I had my family with my mother, father, and brother. Then I got married and joined another family. Then you have your kids and create a new family, and when they all get married and have their own families, hopefully it works out so that it meshes into one. That's kind of the way it has happened here in Kansas City with me.

I've been to a lot of football games and I've done a lot of things out at Arrowhead over the last 21 years since stepping away from the game, but this felt like being welcomed back into the fold. I got the most emotional when I gave my speech at the introduction ceremony. When I talked about family in my speech, the first thing I did was thank Clark and Tavia Hunt for continuing the great tradition that was started by Clark's father, Lamar, who drafted me.

Clark has done an unbelievable job of keeping that family whole, connected, and relevant like the Chiefs organization has been. Then after thanking the Hunt family, I thought about my brothers who were there and the brothers who weren't—my teammates throughout the years. I'm thankful for that special bond, friendship, and brotherhood that we developed over the 11 years that I was there while going through good times and bad.

Going into the locker room every day and going into the weight room in the offseason every day builds those relationships. To be in front of those guys and be honored, I was so grateful that I had that opportunity. After talking about the Hunt family and about my teammates, I had to talk about the Chiefs' fans and Kansas City as a whole. I can't thank Kansas City enough for the way that it took me into their family. My family has grown up and has had such an unbelievable experience living here in Kansas because of the great people and the great atmosphere that is here.

Many athletes talk about why they stay in Kansas City after they're done playing. Most of them stay because it is a great place to raise your family. It's a great place to feel like you're a part of the community. Even though Kansas City is a bigger town, it still has that small-town feel. The Chiefs are a part of that extended family of the Kansas City community.

I had my kids stand up there with me and I told them that they are my treasures, my life, my heart. A lot of people have said over the years that my induction should have happened 10 or

15 years ago, but I'm so thankful that it didn't because my kids now understand the trials and tribulations of being a person in sports. They understand how hard it is, how much dedication it takes, because they've gone through it. It made it that much more special.

Of course, I talked about Sarah, who has been my best friend and my soulmate since we were 18 years old. After every game at Notre Dame, I would search her out and have that communication, sometimes non-verbal, with her. That was a tradition that we started at Notre Dame, and we carried it over to the Chiefs. After every Chiefs game she was able to attend, I did the same thing. I had to make sure that we locked eyes and had a chance to give each other a glance. Whether it was a win or loss, whether I played well or poorly, I made sure that my support system was there. Even though I've been retired for 21 years, every day I have to find some time where we can lock eyes during the day and enjoy each other, what we've done, and what we've had. Being in the Ring of Honor and the Chiefs Hall of Fame brought back a lot of those emotions.

Driving up to that stadium—driving "home"—it felt like being welcomed back. But it was also different. When I drove into the stadium as a player and even in my various roles with the team since then, I had a job to do. But this was my day. This was Tim Grunhard's day that I was granted through all the hard work and dedication, the aches and pains, the wins and losses.

So driving in, I felt that sense of accomplishment, that sense of pride, and the humbling feeling of knowing that your name and your bust would be in the Chiefs Hall of Fame and the Ring of Honor for the rest of your life and even into the lives of your grandkids and even their kids. It meant I was a part of this organization forever.

As a Chiefs player, you feel like you're part of the organization, you feel like it's always going to be there. But when you retire, you realize pretty quickly that while you're still accepted in the community and in the Chiefs organization, you're really not a part of it. This was the first time I felt like I was a part of it again. It was a great feeling and a great honor. Another thing that was different from my days as a player is that I knew that when I drove home that I would feel just as good as I did when I drove in. I wouldn't have the aches and pains. Every morning I still wake up with those aches and pains. It takes a little bit of time to kind of loosen up. Those aches and pains, especially the couple of weeks after the induction ceremony, haven't been as bad. Maybe it's psychological because I felt like I was on cloud nine.

A lot of people, who are given an honor like the one I received, will tell you they never thought they'd have the chance. But I didn't feel that way. The first time I came to Kansas City, I went to Arrowhead Stadium right after the NFL draft for a luncheon with the Chiefs Red Coaters. I walked around the stadium a little bit with general manager Carl Peterson. We took a tour of the offices. He showed me his office and Lamar Hunt's suite. Then we walked out into the stadium, and he pointed up to those names. I looked around, seeing some of the names that I recognized and some of them I didn't recognize. I saw the names and immediately told Carl that my goal was to one day have my name up there. My goal wasn't necessarily to make the Pro Football Hall of Fame. I wanted to have my name in the Ring of Honor. He said that it was a good goal to have and then added, "That's why we drafted you."

Many people have asked me, "When did it really hit you that you were a part of the Chiefs Hall of Fame?" I tell them that it happened when they pulled that curtain down and I saw my name up there. I was able to look over at Sarah, look at my kids, and realize that I was a permanent part of Arrowhead Stadium. It's a crazy, crazy feeling that you're up there with all the greats. It reminded me of walking into that stadium more than 30 years earlier.

As my career went on, I got to know some of those people who had their names on the Ring of Honor and obviously played with some people who later got their names put up there. I am someone who never had a lot of confidence because I've always felt like I had something to prove. So when Carl said, "We drafted you to be a part of this organization for the rest of your life and put your name up on the Ring of Honor," it was an unbelievable feeling for me.

Before every game when I would walk out onto the field, I had certain things that I did. I put my helmet in the same spot in the end zone. I would stretch and do a lot my pregame routine in the same spot. But the one thing I always did when I walked into the stadium was look up at those names and say, "Someday if I can continue to work hard and to dedicate myself and be lucky not to have injuries, then I can have my name up there."

When the curtain was pulled and my name was up there, it became real. It was a great lesson to everybody that if you set your goals high and you believe in yourself, it might take five years, 10 years, or it could even take 31 years. But when it happens, it is a great, great honor.

With four minutes to go in the first half, my family and I went down on the field. My kids had never been on the field during an NFL game. They thought it was really cool to be down on the field and see these big guys running around. One of my daughters said, "It's really scary how big and fast these guys are. Dad, did you really do this against guys this big?"

I said, "Yeah."

In addition to having that moment with my family, I cannot tell you how many people locked eyes with me and were just as happy and excited as I was. They were tearful and they were excited. I looked up into the crowd, and they were just so happy that one of theirs was going into the Ring of Honor. That's the biggest compliment a player can get. I get it all the time from Chiefs fans that I was one of their guys, that I was and always will be a Kansas City Chief.

I've had opportunities to live in other places. I had opportunities to play for different teams, but I made the conscious decision to stay in this community as a part of this organization. To be able to share that with those Chiefs fans—and they know some of the sacrifices I made, and I know some of the sacrifices they made in order to be Chiefs fans—was a great experience.

The last person I brought up in my speech was Sarah because to me she was the most important person. I could see people looking around wondering if I was going to forget to talk about my wife. I got a kick out of that, too. But I got a little choked up talking about her. It took me about 30 seconds to compose myself. But other than that, it was a celebration. I thought about all the things she and I have gone through here in Kansas City while we were away from our immediate families who were in Chicago and New Jersey. It was just us.

At times it was rough around the holidays. We had Thanksgiving dinner with just the two of us. At our first Christmas, we had a camcorder set out. We'd open gifts and talk to the camcorder because we didn't have anyone else here. Those were special moments. I'm so grateful to the Chiefs for giving me the time to share that. I'm so grateful to my teammates and grateful to Kansas City that I was able to reminisce and think how blessed I've been over the years here with this sport.

Football is a game of emotion. In baseball they talk about how you have to be able to take emotion out of it to be successful. You have to "try easier." You kind of have to dismiss the emotion. It's probably true in a lot of other sports as well. But in football you want to be emotional. You want to be personally invested. Football is predicated on being tougher, stronger, and in control of the other team probably more so than other sports.

The other thing is that football is really hard. You're doing things that your mind is telling you that you really shouldn't do. Throwing your body in front of a 300-pound man and letting him knock you over is not a natural thing to do. To go and tackle somebody running at full speed or to jump up in the air and let somebody hit you in the back, those are all things that your mind is saying, "No, don't do that."

There are points in every game and there are points in every season that you couldn't do it for yourself. You have to go through training camp. It's a grind to have 16 games per season, not counting preseason—now they have 17 regular-season games—and there are times where mentally you just can't do it. That's when you look at your family and your teammates. When it got really hard, I would look over and I would see Dave Szott and Will Shields or I would see Joe Montana, Dave Krieg, or Rich Gannon and I would think, *I can do it for these guys.*

As an offensive lineman, you're basically a bodyguard. You're taking bullets for the quarterback. There were times when I was out of position and I said to myself, *The quarterback's going to get hit or I'm going to take a hit.* I chose to take a hit, to throw my body in the way, knowing I was going to pay for it. That's football.

It's just such a great microcosm of life because we all have to "convert." There are all these fourth-down situations that you've got to convert with family, with marriages, with friends, with a job, and with everything else, and it's just a great way to learn a lesson that sometimes you do things for the betterment of other people over yourself, and that's how you get through life.

In the fourth quarter when you're exhausted and you're beat up and tired, you have to find something to drive you to keep going. As the center, my hands would be so swollen that I could barely touch them, and I had to grab the football. You can't do it for yourself. It's a weird thing. That's why it is so important to have that bond and emotional connection that you have with the team. That's why football is the greatest team sport because not only do you depend on the other 10 guys in order to have success, but you also depend on them to get you through.

When I looked at the eyes of that Chiefs Hall of Fame bust, it was like a reflection to me, like looking into a mirror. People have said their busts are objects that had dead eyes, but they weren't to me. I looked into the eyes of that bust and I saw the struggle, the emotions, the pride, and the love of the game in the eyes of that bust, which was weird. I could not keep my eyes off the eyes of that bust. I don't know if there is any other Hall of Famer who has had that feeling. I've never had a bust like that before. But to me, those eyes told me so much. It was like saying, "Job well done."

The rest of this book is the story told through those eyes.

Born Hungry

I WAS BORN HUNGRY. I WAS NEVER THE STAR ATHLETE—EVEN IN my own family. There's just me and my brother, and my brother is four years older than I am. Because of that age difference, I was always following him in school. When I was going into my freshman year of high school, he had just graduated. He set the precedent. Dan was a superstar athlete; he played baseball and got a scholarship to play at Northwestern University outside of Chicago. He had a long career in the minor leagues in the California Angels system.

For good or bad, my father made us very competitive with each other, which turned out to not make the best relationship. Everything we did, we were judged. My dad was a very competitive person. He felt the only way he could get his kids to get to the level where we both ended up was to challenge us competitively against each other and against other people in the neighborhood. He held us up to a standard that I felt I could never live up to because my brother was four years older.

Even though my brother and my father were both very supportive, in their minds you were either a winner or loser. There was nothing in between. I always felt like it was impossible for me to gain any oxygen in the room when it came to athletics. But that's on me.

My brother often included me with all the buddies in the neighborhood. We'd play football, basketball, and baseball in the backyards and the alleys in Chicago. They never took it easy on me. So, I didn't have a lot of success, as you can imagine. Success was limited, so I always felt second fiddle. I always felt like I just could not live up to the standards that were being set.

Maybe the reason I chose to pursue football was that my brother did not play high school football. He didn't play any other sport. He played a little basketball, but he never played football, which is kind of how I gravitated toward it. I was a pretty good baseball player growing up, but I always kind of wanted to get out of the shadow of my brother. He was an A student, and I wasn't. He was an all-state baseball player, and I wasn't. So I tried to keep my own path and become a football player. It kind of got me a little bit of separation, which I felt I needed.

My father was a Chicago policeman. He worked midnights from 11:00 PM to about 8:00 AM. He'd go home and take a nap and then he would coach our baseball teams. Then he would have dinner and take another nap. The only time I ever saw him was when he was my baseball coach.

I was competing more for my dad's attention than I was competing on the field. And yet the way I competed for my dad's attention was to be successful on the field. My father passed away from cancer during my rookie year in the NFL. He came to one Kansas City Chiefs game. And he said, "You know, this is a pretty good life for you, but it's no Notre Dame." So even though I reached the pinnacle of playing in the NFL, his pinnacle for me was something different.

Growing up on the south side of Chicago, there were only two teams. One was Notre Dame, and the other was the Chicago Bears. On Notre Dame Saturdays, my mom would close the windows because my father would let out so many expletives. His line was, "The officials are cheating the Catholics."

He loved the Bears and loved Notre Dame football. That's all there was. We didn't bother my dad on Saturday. He sat in his chair and watched the Notre Dame game. Then on Sundays, it was the same thing with the Bears. So that's how we grew up. But you know there was that passion. He had a lot of passion when it came to those two teams. And really in the whole neighborhood, that's just the way it was. That passion was passed along to my brother and me, and it caused a lot of heartache and headache between us. It was a tough way to be raised, but it worked. He got two Division I athletes and two professional athletes out of his two sons. That just doesn't happen very often.

Sometimes we had to look for competition. Growing up in the south side of Chicago, the heart of White Sox country, we were Cubs fans. It was never easy because all our friends and all the people we hung around with were all Sox fans. It almost felt like my father did it on purpose to keep us uncomfortable and on edge. I think his goal in life was to get us out of our comfort zone. When he did that, he felt like he had success that day. He thought you could not grow unless you were uncomfortable. He thought you could not become the man that he wanted you to be unless you were uncomfortable. It was hard to live uncomfortable all the time, but I can't argue with the results. Either you grew or you died in a competitive sense. There was no in between.

In a way my mom was the same. She was extremely competitive, but she demonstrated it differently. She went to all our games and she wanted us to be our best. She would say, "What a great game you played" even if we didn't. She was the counterpoint to the man who was standing on the other side of the room.

I also grew up across the street from a country club. It was almost like there was a wall. It was called the Ridge Country Club, and we lived right off the 17th tee. In the summers we'd sit in the backyard and watch everybody play golf, knowing we didn't belong. The first thing we wanted to do was go see the girls at the pool. But we couldn't go to the pool; we literally and figuratively didn't belong.

I think that my dad liked that. He wanted me to be uncomfortable. I'm sure he probably could have found a way for us to join that country club. But that wasn't going to happen. We were going to earn our way to those kinds of things; he was not going to give us that stuff. I remember everyone going to the 7-Eleven to get a candy bar and a Coke. I didn't have any money. I would go and look for pop bottles so I could bring them in for the refund of five or 10 cents. If you found five or six of those, that was enough to get your Coke for that day. That was just the way it was. I didn't feel like I was neglected. I didn't feel like I was being held back. I never felt like I was poor. I just wasn't given things. It made me work harder.

I earned my way. I earned my respect on the field, I earned my respect in the park, I earned my respect with my father. I held myself to a higher standard athletically. It didn't matter if I thought I was having success. I always felt like I could have done something better. I felt like I could have gotten an extra hit, made that extra block, or made that next tackle. That was that hunger that was instilled in me from the start.

That probably wasn't the healthiest way to grow up. But it was the only way we knew how to do it. And in our neighborhood, there were only two people who became professional athletes, and that's my brother and me. So my father must have known what he was doing.

It didn't make for the easiest of childhoods, but in the long run, my dad was just like every tough coach or every tough teacher. When you look back, those are the teachers and the coaches that really made you into something.

I think of my college coach Lou Holtz, who was the ultimate psychologist. He found your weakness and he exploited that weakness. For me, the weakness was I was a pleaser. I always wanted to please and I never felt like I was doing enough. I never felt like I was pleasing my coach, my father, or my teachers. I always felt like I wasn't quite there. And he knew that. There are many examples of him pushing those buttons on me. Going into my senior year at Notre Dame, Lou was talking about all the guys who were going to get drafted and have a good chance to play in the NFL. He put my name down on his list and said, "I don't know about this guy."

I had just come off an unbelievable year when I was a second-team All-American. But he knew that if he gave me that compliment, I might rest on my laurels or take a deep breath and rest. He knew that I just couldn't do that. That's the way I was motivated. He figured that out. It started with my dad. I was like a horse with a carrot. I always had that carrot dangling in front of me. Yeah, I had success, but I wasn't as successful or well-acclaimed as my brother. I played at Notre Dame, but I was the last guy offered a scholarship in my class. I had a chance to play in the NFL, but I wasn't a sure-fire pro. I always had that carrot in front of me.

For my third birthday in the spring of 1971, my mom's sister bought me a football helmet. She went to a sporting goods store in Albuquerque, New Mexico, to purchase it. The Chiefs had won the Super Bowl in January 1970, so sporting goods stores around the country carried Chiefs stuff. My aunt had no idea about the Chiefs, Notre Dame, or anything else about football. She just wanted to get me a gift she thought I'd like. So she bought me a Chiefs helmet.

I cried. I thought there were only two teams in the world: Notre Dame and the Bears. Obviously, it wasn't a Bears helmet, so I wanted a Notre Dame helmet. Even at the age of three, I knew the two teams that I was allowed to root for in that house. But at the age of three, there was a foreshadowing of my football future.

All I remember was thinking, *This isn't a Notre Dame helmet.* According to my mom, tears streamed down, and disappointment showed on my face. Knowing how I loved Notre Dame, my dad found some gold spray paint and transformed the Chiefs helmet into a Notre Dame helmet. Needless to say, that helmet and I were inseparable that whole summer until the paint started to wear off and the Chiefs red started to bleed through. Talk about karma. Who would have known that the only two teams I've ever played for in my adult football life were constant companions with me in the summer of 1971? I wore that helmet everywhere. My mom would tell me I couldn't wear it to church. But I would cry until she let me wear it to church.

The son of a police officer and a nurse, I was dedicated, persistent, and driven. I was the son of a man who believed I would only grow if I was uncomfortable. I was also the son of a woman who would tell me I did great whether or not I did. Actually, both things helped me gain the confidence that it took to play Division I football and to play in the NFL for 11 years.

They both helped me fight through Dan Saleaumua in practice or Cortez Kennedy in a game.

I faced tougher fights trying to be as good as my brother. Looking at it realistically, my brother Dan was probably not the athlete I was because I had more professional success than he did. I've thought about when I was able to convince myself that I actually had some potential. When did the toughness that my dad instilled, the encouragement that my mom gave me, and the desire to achieve what my brother did finally click?

I think it started early in my career at St. Laurence High School. I'll never forget my freshman year. I really wasn't starting or even playing much. I couldn't understand that because I thought that I was good enough to do that. It was one of those times where I said to myself, *I'm going to show you.* I was playing defensive line at that time, and my teammates kept complimenting me. They were always saying, "Hey, you're pretty good."

I didn't realize that, but in my sophomore year, I started to play really well. At the end of the year, a couple of sophomores got brought up to the varsity, but I did not. I was slapped back down into my reality. The other two guys, Jeff Pearson and Paul Glonek, both ended up getting scholarships to play Division I football, so they deserved it. But I sat in the stands and watched those two guys play. I was thinking that was where I should have been. I had to find a way to work harder or dig deeper, find a way to do something extra to get out of my comfort zone in order to be where I need to be.

Those series of three steps forward and two steps back kept happening. It happened even in my recruiting process. I wasn't recruited by Notre Dame because Gerry Faust thought I was too small. But Holtz recruited me to Minnesota. I didn't want to go to Minnesota. The only place I wanted to go was Notre Dame, and the Fighting Irish were not recruiting me. I was devastated. I got scholarship offers to Texas, Nebraska, South Carolina, Kansas, and Missouri. But Notre Dame didn't want me. So when Lou

Holtz took the Notre Dame job, I was hoping that he would carry over that scholarship from Minnesota, and he did.

Had all that not happened with Lou, I probably would have ended up at either Nebraska or South Carolina. Nebraska coach Tom Osborne came to my house. Coach Osborne is very shy and introverted. He was hardly saying a word. His recruiting coordinator was going through the whole thing. And Osborne said at the end, "We would love you to come and play for the University of Nebraska." And I thought, *Man, this guy is really cool.* He was the opposite of my dad. My dad was always brash and upfront. And this guy was calm, cool, and collected. I thought Osborne was a cool guy.

And then I went down to South Carolina. The reason why I was considering going to South Carolina was because it was just a beautiful place with beautiful girls and unbelievable football. I went to the South Carolina–Clemson game, and I said, "This is the place for me."

I took visits to Kansas and to Missouri because we used to travel to the Lake of the Ozarks in the summer when I was growing up. I figured if I liked the Lake of the Ozarks, I might as well go to one of the schools in the area. But I knew that neither of those places was where I wanted to go. When I called Lou Holtz and told him I wanted to accept the scholarship offer, I thought he'd be pretty excited about it, but he didn't sound like he was that excited about me accepting the scholarship. I think he offered me the scholarship because he already had a relationship with me. I think he really wanted someone better but ran out of time in the recruiting process.

I never enjoyed the recruiting process. I neither enjoyed recruiting when I was being recruited nor when I was a college coach. It's not a great process. One of the best ways to survive recruiting—and anything related to an athletic career for that matter—is to have somebody who believes in you. And I had one in a buddy of mine who was my main competitor. We were inseparable. He was my best friend. His name is Dan Benoit. (We used to call him "Bah.")

We'd constantly have battles. We'd play each other in one-on-one basketball. When you took a shot, you had to call out who you were. He knew who Michael Jordan and Patrick Ewing were before I had any idea who these guys were. I was yelling out "Reggie Theus" and guys like Dr. J, and he was yelling out college guys. We were so competitive. We played this game we called "the ground ball game." There was a sewer that sat in the backyard. If you can hit the sewer cover, you never knew where the ball was going to bounce. It was a big thing to try to get the ball by the other guy.

He was always there. He was the best basketball player on our team. He was the running back on our football team. He was a really good baseball player. We pushed each other. We were more like brothers than my own brother and I were because of the age difference. Once again, it was built on competition. We were very competitive with each other, but we were also very supportive of each other. And we did everything together. I needed somebody like that between the ages of 10 and 18.

I recently met a woman who was in the 1984 Olympics in synchronized swimming and won the gold medal. I told her, "You personally are responsible for me playing in the NFL."

In 1984 the Russians pulled out of the Olympics in Los Angeles because we had boycotted the 1980 Olympics in Russia. Without their main rival, the Americans won nearly every gold medal. There were very few sports that the U.S. didn't win something. Well, in 1984, McDonald's had a promotion. When you bought a meal, you got a little postcard. You pulled a tab, and if the American team or individual won a gold medal, you got a free Big Mac. Bah and I would go and buy a Big Mac and get a card. We'd pull the card and then go through the drive-through and get another one because we probably just won a gold medal in whatever sport was on the card.

Going into my sophomore year, I put on 25 pounds in one summer. It was a growth spurt, but I got big. I went from 5'7" and 167 pounds my freshman year in high school to almost 6'2" and 250 pounds by my junior year. I put on almost 100 pounds in high school and grew about six inches. But I told her it was because she won a gold medal in synchronized swimming.

Bah and I always found a way to be competitive. And we're close to this day. He was the best man in my wedding. Whenever I was feeling kind of down and out, I'd give him a call. And he'd always be there. I needed somebody, and Bah was the guy who was there. He believed in me, he understood me. He pushed me, he never would let me win anything. That was the stuff that I craved.

There always seemed to be somebody who had my back, somebody who spurred me on. I think about my Pop Warner coach John Hook. If you weren't hustling, he was another one of those guys who'd make you run a lap around the park. We'd do leg lifts, and if your legs touched the ground, you'd have to start over again.

I didn't want to go to practice one day for Hook. I was there, but I made up an excuse that my mom and dad wanted me to go to dinner. First of all, Coach Hook knew that my dad would never schedule a family dinner during practice. So he knew what was going on. My competition at this point was a guy named Larry. When I was walking off the field, Coach Hook blew the whistle, stopped the practice, and said, "Larry, we're gonna put you at running back."

All the guys were trying to tackle the big guy. I never scored a touchdown in my whole career. In four years of grade school, four years of high school, four years of college, and 11 years in the NFL, I never scored a touchdown. For me the idea of carrying a football and running in for a touchdown was everything. So I said, "No, no, I can stay; I can do that."

But Coach Hook said, "No, you've got to go to dinner."

As I was walking off that field, I learned a valuable lesson. If you're not there, there's always going to be somebody to take your spot. Somebody else is going to have that success, have that fun. That's one of the main reasons I played 120 games in a row in the NFL. I never missed practice or came out of a game. I was definitely afraid that somebody was going to come in and take my spot. Somebody was going to do something that I could have done to make the difference. Those are the little lessons that you learn when you're in seventh grade or in Pop Warner football that you carry on the rest of your life. I remember walking off that field and crying because I didn't have the opportunity to do something as simple as running the football.

Overcoming others' opinions goes back to eighth grade. St. Laurence High School had an eighth-grade game, where all the eighth-grade boys, who were going to try to play sports, ran sprints and went to the weight room. I never lifted weights until I got to high school, so I had no idea how to do any of that stuff. I went in there and tried to bench the bar, and it came down on my chest. I was embarrassed. I couldn't do a pull up and I could barely do a push up. And I could hear the snickers and the laughs. I think my brother probably got me an invite to this thing because he was a senior at the school and was a really good athlete. But I was a dismal failure. I knew at that point that I had to find a way to have some success, get stronger, and work harder. Those are the things I always knew. But it wasn't just overcoming others' opinions. I also had to overcome my own opinion of what my limits were.

Going into my freshman year at Notre Dame, I sat at the dinner table with my dad a couple of days before I was supposed to report. I told him, "I don't know if I can compete with those guys."

I was doubting myself. I was questioning whether I could do it. My dad just said, "If you think you can't, you won't." He was making me tougher.

Coming into the NFL, the same thing happened. Even though I was an All-American and a second-round draft choice, I didn't think I could compete. I was afraid I was going to get cut. One of the other offensive linemen said, "You know, there was a guy who was a second-round draft pick who got cut a couple years ago." I don't know if that actually happened; I think he was trying to get in my head so I wouldn't be overconfident. But at that point, I thought for sure I'd be next. When I made the team, I was surprised. That was just the way I thought. I could not believe that I was going to play in the NFL, I could not believe that I was going to be wearing a Chiefs uniform and playing in Arrowhead Stadium, making a living playing football. I just always felt like I didn't have it. And I had to prove to myself that I could do it over and over again. That was a process I went through every time. It's true with anything I do—even to this day. I even have a horrible fear of reading out loud. I've got to do reads for radio spots. Even in crowds, I have a little bit of anxiety in front of people. I have to kind of dig deep to find that energy to go ahead and do those things. It's just the way that I was built.

That's probably what made me such a perfect fit for the Chiefs. The Chiefs fans are blue-collar tough, no-nonsense people. I saw my dad in Chiefs fans. When I first got to Kansas City, I felt like I owed it to them to get out of my comfort zone and prove to those people that this No. 61 *can* do it. That's the reason I always ran to the line of scrimmage from the huddle and finished the play down the field. When our running back was tackled, I was always the first one to pick him up.

I did all those things because I was trying to please the fans. I wanted the fans to feel like I was worthy of being cheered. It all kind of circles back to trying to be a pleaser. Pleasing my father was a lot like pleasing the Chiefs fans. The Chiefs fans kind of replaced my father. They were there when my father passed away during my rookie year. I saw a lot of their spirit, a lot of their toughness, a lot of their enthusiasm, and a lot of the same traits in Chiefs fans that I saw in my dad. So, it really was a perfect fit for me.

I spent my entire 11-year career hungry to show the Chiefs fans that I belonged. From the very first snap of the Minnesota Vikings game to the last snap against the Atlanta Falcons, I always felt like I owed them something extra. And I had to find another gear to get out of my comfort zone and give the Chiefs fans what they deserved. A lot of that was exactly what I did when I was two and three years old.

I don't know if it would have been the same way in San Diego. I don't know if it would have been the same way in Tampa, New York, or even Chicago. If I had been drafted by the Bears, it might have been too close. I had to get out. I had to find my own path. Maybe I had to escape Chicago. I would have had relatives and friends and coaches there. I didn't have anybody when I got to Kansas City. Sarah and I were engaged when I got here, and she lived in Chicago for a couple years. I had nobody here but Dave Szott. I had to find a way to excel when things were tough. I had to learn how to grow when I was uncomfortable. That was what propelled me to become a Ring of Honor football player in Kansas City.

It was a perfect storm.

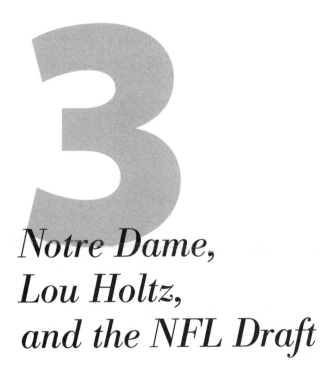

Notre Dame,
Lou Holtz,
and the NFL Draft

THE RECRUITING PROCESS BACK IN THE 1980S REALLY DIDN'T
start until the summer before your senior year. It kind of built
up during the season, and then right after the season, you learned
about who liked you and who was going to recruit you. I'm sure
that anybody who was recruited during that era would remember that high school coaches would never give you the letters or
any of the different mailings that schools would send you during
the season. They'd wait until the season was over.

Most guys really didn't have much of an idea who was recruiting them. But I knew because of Tom Lemming, who was a
recruiting guru and became a huge recruiting expert for ESPN.
He published a newsletter for the city of Chicago, which was a
recruiting hotbed at the time. He was very close with Gerry Faust,
the head coach at Notre Dame. He made his bones helping Notre
Dame recruit some big-name guys all over the country. Lemming
told me I wasn't being recruited by Notre Dame at all because I
was too short. Faust had a rule that his offensive linemen had to
be at least 6'4"—and preferably 6'5"—to play for him. Obviously,
I wasn't that size, so I was too short for Notre Dame.

It really hurt me because there were other Division I schools
who were interested in me. They were pretty good football programs who were at that time better than Notre Dame and they
had no issue with my size. There was nothing I could do about

getting taller. All I could do was work harder and earn a reputation and gain a name for myself through playing my senior year.

There were four or five other guys in my high school and four or five other guys who I played against in the Chicago Catholic League who were offered scholarships to Notre Dame. I thought I was at least as good as, if not better than, those guys. Maybe Coach Faust just didn't like me.

It frustrated me because I couldn't control it. I had a lot of bitterness toward Notre Dame. That whole year, I remember rooting against Notre Dame. It was sacrilegious in my house to root against Notre Dame. My dad said, "This is bigger than you. This has always been your team, your school, and you're rooting against them because you're not getting something you want."

But it was like being shunned by that girl you wanted to date. That's the way I felt. As a good teammate, I should have been proud and happy for those guys who got that opportunity. But I wasn't happy for them. I was bitter. It may have been small of me, but I was jealous. When I was running around at three or four years old and could put a football helmet on, that was the school I wanted to attend. Because I wasn't given that opportunity, I was jealous and I was not happy for those guys. I was happy that they were going to play college football somewhere, but I was not happy it was for Notre Dame. Everybody was talking about the guys who were going to Notre Dame, and I wasn't included. That was kind of a slam on me.

I always felt that nothing was ever given to me. I had to earn what I got, which made me into who I am. When I was given what I wanted, I was happy again, which is not the way you should go about life. But I probably wasn't the best teammate my senior year in high school. I learned to be a good teammate through my years at Notre Dame. You've got to learn to put the needs of other people—your teammates—above your own to earn any kind of success.

Now, to be fair to Notre Dame, I wasn't really being recruited heavily by anybody else either. But one guy from the University of Minnesota called me in July or August of the summer before my senior year. His name was Lou Holtz. I think he was a little bit ahead of the game. He said, "I want to recruit you, I want to offer you a scholarship, I want to send my assistant coach to come and see you play."

As my high school year finished and I got all the letters and offers, there was nothing from Notre Dame. Lemming said, "You're just going to have to *settle* for going to a different school. There are a lot of great schools interested: the University of Minnesota, South Carolina, Nebraska, or Texas."

It's somewhat funny, but I viewed it as having to settle to play football at Nebraska or Texas. But that was my mind-set. Maybe it was kind of immature, but that was the way I was raised: there was Notre Dame and everybody else. I did learn from recruiting visits that there is other life out there, but that didn't change my dream of playing for the Fighting Irish.

The last game of the 1985 season, the Faust-coached Fighting Irish went down to Miami and got shellacked. The rumor started quickly that he was going to get fired. I didn't know if that was true, and it probably was a bit presumptuous to think that would change things for me, but the sun started coming out. Maybe somebody would take that job who didn't look at height and would be willing to recruit me.

Walking on at Notre Dame and trying to earn a scholarship was never a possibility. My parents couldn't afford to send me to Notre Dame. It really wasn't an option for me. It was either a scholarship or nothing—not just for Notre Dame but for any school. Fast forward to my son, Colin, who, like me, really wanted to go to Notre Dame and play football. He had some scholarships to some other places, but his parents could afford to send him to Notre Dame. That wasn't an opportunity for me. If I was going to college, I had to get a football scholarship.

When Faust ended up getting fired, there were two big names who were brought up as possible replacements. One was Forrest Gregg, who was with the Green Bay Packers at that time. The other one was Lou. A light bulb went off in my head that he was the guy who recruited me to Minnesota. Maybe, just maybe, he might recruit me to Notre Dame. He offered me a scholarship to Minnesota, but it wasn't automatic that I would be offered a scholarship at Notre Dame. When Lou took the job, I didn't hear from him right away. I did talk to George Stewart, who was the recruiting coordinator at Minnesota and was finishing up the job there.

Holtz didn't take the Notre Dame job until early January, and Signing Day was the first Wednesday of February. Holtz started the recruiting process, and Coach Stewart stayed at Minnesota to finish that recruiting cycle before moving to Notre Dame. He knew that he was moving on with Holtz, but he didn't tell me. His demeanor changed from how great Minnesota was to how great Holtz was.

About two or three weeks later, I was working at Walgreens in the middle of January. My manager came up and said, "You have a phone call." Who gets a phone call at Walgreens? My parents were not going to call me there, so I figured it was one of my friends saying, "Hey, let's go out. We're going to have a party."

So I got on the phone, and the voice on the other end said, "This is Lou Holtz at the University of Notre Dame." I paused;

this wasn't Coach Holtz. How would he find me at Walgreens? So I said sarcastically, "Who is this?"

He made it clear that he really was Lou Holtz, and at that point, I thought I just burned my bridge to ever play at Notre Dame. But he understood, I guess, and he offered me an opportunity to visit the campus the next weekend. He said, "I liked you at Minnesota and I like you here at Notre Dame. I'd like to sit down and talk to you about Notre Dame." I wasn't offered a scholarship per se at that point, but I was offered a visit. I was going to get a chance.

I went on the visit with my parents. All the way on the drive there, my parents kept telling me, "It's your decision. We're not the ones going to school, we're not the one going to play four years of football. You go where you want to go."

Maybe they thought I wasn't going to get a scholarship offer and they were trying to prepare me. Maybe they didn't want me to be able to blame them if I went there and disliked it. But they insisted that it was up to me.

The very first thing that happened when we got to South Bend was walking into Coach Holtz's office. He offered to show me around the school and then offered me a scholarship. We all walked out of there happy. At least for a little while.

South Bend, Indiana, in January is horrible. It was boring. And it was cold. I had taken a trip to South Carolina where there were plenty of southern belles. We went out to all these cool college bars and we went to a dorm party. I had a great time in the community. But it wasn't Notre Dame, so I was torn. The next morning, I got up and met my parents for breakfast. As we were getting ready to leave and have our checkout meeting with Coach Holtz, my parents said, "So when are you going to commit to Notre Dame?"

I said, "I thought this was my decision."

They said, "You're going to Notre Dame."

So I took a couple of days and called Lou and said, "I'm going to play football for Notre Dame."

It was weird; I didn't feel like he was that excited when I committed. He said, "Okay, we'll send you some information and we'll talk with you later." I was the last guy offered to Notre Dame in that class.

We had to report to campus in the middle of July, a little bit earlier than they do now. We had a couple of weeks of workouts before two-a-days camp, and all the freshmen came in a day or two earlier than everybody else. My mom was standing there, crying because she was letting go of her baby. Coach Stewart saw her. He went over and put his arm around her. He knew my mom from the recruiting process. He said, "Don't worry, I'll take care of your baby. He'll be all right."

My mom was very thankful to Coach Stewart for going out of his way. She felt better leaving because of that.

Right after the parents left, the varsity guys came in. When you're an 18-year-old kid and these 21- or 22-year-old guys come in with their beards developed, you feel like a little kid. How was I going to compete against those guys? They were men.

As the 1986 recruiting class, we felt pretty good about ourselves because we were the first recruiting class that Lou put together. Granted, he only had about a month and a half to put this class together. He didn't have the whole year or six months or whatever the schools have for the recruiting process. But we still felt pretty good about ourselves. We believed we were the class that would restore the tradition at Notre Dame. Lou walked in and said, "Everybody get your feet on the ground, sit up straight, get your pens and paper out, and take notes." Then he said, "I want only the guys I recruited to stand up right now."

We all kind of looked at each other and thought, *Here we go. Lou will say that this is the class that we're going use to build a foundation of Notre Dame football. You guys had your opportunity over the last four or five years, didn't take advantage of it. I'm here now, and these are my guys and I'm proud of these guys that I've brought in.*

It's almost like there were angels singing in the background, and the light from heaven was on us. But Lou looked at us, looked down at his veteran guys, looked back up, and said, "Let me tell you something: if I had one more month, none of your asses would be here."

He pretty much put us in our places. He was saying: don't think you've got this figured out. Don't think you're anything special. Don't think that because you're my first recruiting class that you're going to have any kind of dispensation cause. It ain't going to happen. You're going to have to earn it.

He was really tough on our class—tougher than on any other class. He set us straight at that point. Fast forward three years later, that was the nucleus of that junior class that won the national championship in 1988 and won 24 of our final 25 games. That class really came together. But he made it really rough on us.

I had the opportunity to dress for the first game against No. 3 Michigan, which was not a given for a freshman. It's a little bit of an honor to dress for home games because you can only have a certain number of guys on the sideline. I was the second-team long snapper and probably third-team guard as well. I remember running onto that field. It was a great feeling with a lot of excitement, a lot of pomp and circumstance. It's just an unbelievable feeling to be standing on the sideline at a Notre Dame football game.

I had never been to a Notre Dame football game until I ran out onto that field. That was the first game I ever saw in person. I had watched countless games on TV, but I never had the opportunity to go until I dressed for that first game. As I look back on it, that was a great experience. My first time in that stadium on gameday was a day in which I was going to play in the game.

That rush wore off quickly. As the year went on, I realized I was a long way from being on the field. It kind of hurt. I wanted to play. I was never satisfied with just being there. I always wanted to be a part of it. I learned a valuable lesson at that point that I really carried all the way through my football career: if you're ever given an opportunity, you've got to take advantage of it. Don't ever, ever, ever take it for granted because you could lose it.

I did not like standing and watching. That was the only game in my career that I was in full uniform and didn't play a snap. That was tough. I remember coming out after the game, which we lost to Michigan when our kicker missed a field-goal attempt in the final minute. I was kind of embarrassed that I didn't play. My mom, my dad, and my brother came to the game, and I didn't get an opportunity to play. I felt bad that everybody made the effort to come and see me, and they only saw me standing on the sideline. There were games that I went to that Colin didn't get to play. I loved every second of it. Just seeing him on the sideline—that was good enough for me. But I didn't understand that at that time. So I learned a valuable lesson about consistency and taking advantage of opportunities.

The next week we played at Michigan State, and that was the first time I got into a game. It doesn't matter whether you're busing to a game or flying to a game, the saying is "You've got to earn a way onto the bus." All offseason and all summer camp, the coaches talked about who was going to get on the bus. I didn't know whether Lou trusted me or maybe didn't like some of the snaps from the first-team snapper in the Michigan game. But he told me, "You're going to be our long snapper in the Michigan State game. Go about your business and let's do it right."

So I got on the bus and traveled to East Lansing, Michigan. I remember being really nervous and seeing the green jerseys of the Michigan State guys, the white stripe on the helmets. I was just praying that the offense didn't sputter so I'd have to go out there and snap for a punt. Well, the first series was a three-and-out. I ran out on that field hoping to not hear what they call "the moan." Snappers—or even quarterbacks when they're being hit—can't always see what happens. You listen for the moan. And the moan is that sound the crowd makes when the guy snaps the ball, and it bounces or goes over the punter's head.

I snapped my first one and ran off the field as fast as I could. I just didn't want to hear the moan. I didn't hear it. The snap went straight to the punter, and he got the punt away. The rest is history. I did the long snapping all four years at Notre Dame. They generally didn't have guys who just long snapped. I'd be in the middle of a series; we'd go three and out. I'd take my gloves off, throw them on the side, and snap it.

The one thing that I really did to make a name for myself was being one of the fastest guys on the punt team. You might not believe that, but I led the team in tackles as a freshman. Nobody blocked me because nobody thought I could get down there. People would come up to me and say, "You're that long snapper. You really get down the field fast." So that was kind of my claim to fame my freshman year. I always busted my butt down the field to see if I could go make the play.

People who started following me with the Kansas City Chiefs are probably surprised to know that I never played center at Notre Dame. The only time I was at the center position was when I was long snapping. Otherwise, I played guard. I had kind of an emergency throw-in deal at Michigan my sophomore year where I had to play a series at center because our starter got dinged up, and we had nobody else. But I never really practiced at center. The only time I centered the ball was on kicks and punts.

There were a couple of other notable games from my freshman year. The first game was against Alabama and All-American linebacker Cornelius Bennett. He was one of the best outside linebackers/defensive ends in the history of college football. He ended up being the No. 2 overall pick in the 1987 draft the following spring. We played in Alabama, and it felt like it was 120 degrees. We were playing in the old War Memorial Stadium in Birmingham. The turf was just boiling hot. During the third quarter, our right tackle whiffed on a block, and Bennett got around the corner and laid out quarterback Steve Beuerlein. The ball went flying. It was a picture-perfect sack. If you walk into Alabama's stadium today, there is a painting of that sack. Right after that play, Lou said, "Grunhard, get him" and he pulled the right tackle and put me in the game. All of a sudden, here was this freshman playing against this all-American linebacker. I had no chance. They rolled out away from my side a lot.

I basically just got in the way. Bennett threw me around, and I was just hanging on for dear life. I was just trying to do whatever I could do to not totally embarrass myself and get anybody killed. It was tough. It was kind of a low point for me. I wondered if I was going to be able to compete at that level. I'd played some games before where I felt like I could compete, but when I competed against the best defensive player in college football,

I went in intimidated and scared. I had no idea about any kind of success. It showed.

Fast forward a little bit to a *Monday Night Football* game in 1991—my second season in the NFL—against the Buffalo Bills. I had to go up against Bennett again. I was just getting into the prime of my NFL career, but so was Bennett. He was playing for Buffalo. The starting inside linebacker, Darryl Talley, got hurt, so they had to move Bennett to the inside. He wasn't comfortable there. He was a quick guy and he liked to have space to move around. There isn't a lot of space at the inside linebacker position. As everybody remembers, we just kicked the crap out of Buffalo in that game. I kicked the crap out of Bennett in that game, too. He couldn't escape. I got my paws on him and I drove him everywhere. I wasn't cheap-shotting him, but I certainly wasn't helping him off the pile.

The other game that sticks out from my freshman year was when we went down to Baton Rouge, Louisiana, to play LSU. Lou said that it was going to be something special. He had coached against LSU when he coached at Arkansas. He knew it was going to be an unforgettable experience. That place was crazy. Holtz told us that the sellout crowds there would get so loud that it would register on the Richter scale. He also said it was the only time he would accept us smelling like liquor on the football field. We all giggled about that. We didn't know what he was talking about until we went down the tunnel, and 300 beers came pouring down on top of our team as we walked out. That was a christening of our gladiator battle against the LSU Tigers. They also had a live tiger in a cage right at the end of the tunnel. I think they used some kind of electric prod to make the tiger roar at you right when you walked up. It scared the crap out of you. I was this kid from the south side of Chicago, and all of a sudden, there was this tiger roaring at me in my ear. That's pretty intimidating.

I got to play a little bit in the game and I tore the meniscus in my knee in the fourth quarter. I had to have surgery the following Monday. That was the first of my many knee surgeries. The final game of the season was the next weekend on the road at Southern California. Because of the surgery, I wasn't going to be able to play. I wanted to go to California. I'd never been to California. I knew that USC was the big rival and I wanted to go. So I hatched a scheme.

Lou had a rule that if you weren't playing, you didn't travel with the team. There were no "tourists" on our "business trips." I knew the rule, but I figured I'd give myself one shot. I went to his office (on crutches) and sat down. He said, "How can I help you?"

I said, "Coach, I know you have a rule that there are no tourists, no spectators on the sideline with the team, but I've never been to California. I know we're going to play this USC rivalry for the next three years. I really want to learn what this rivalry is all about. I want to get a feel for what I need to do in the next three years in order to give you an opportunity to win football games against USC."

I thought he was going to say, "That's a great idea." In my mind, as an 18-year-old kid, it was a great sell job.

He said, "Nope, I'm not taking you. You know my rules. You follow my rules."

So I had to go home and watch the game at home on Thanksgiving.

The funny thing about it is that it must have made an impression on him because every time I see him or if I'm in the audience and he knows I'm there when he's doing a speech, he always brings up that story about me asking to go to California. It didn't work, but it made an impression.

Lou made an impression on everyone who ever played for him. For one thing, his practices were legendary. No matter what the weather was like, he wanted us to give our all during practice. The summer before my senior year, we were coming off the national championship, but he didn't want us to rest on our laurels. Every day in training camp it was well over 95 degrees. It was hot and humid. It was miserable and it was tough. Every day he would tell us he called Michigan coach Bo Schembechler and said, "It's hot out there. If you give your guys a day off, I'll give my guys a day off. And Bo said, 'No, we're practicing.'"

He didn't call Schembechler. That whole summer it was all about "Bo said no." Coach Holtz was always the psychologist. His practices were tough.

My teammate, Chris Zorich, only had one speed, which was great as a teammate. It's great when you're playing on Saturdays. But in practice it gets old quickly. As the season went on, I got more and more sore. The last thing you wanted to do was bust your butt in practice.

Unfortunately, I drew the short straw and I had to go against Zorich every day. In the long run, it really helped me and made me the player I was. In one particular practice, Zorich was just taking it to me. I was a senior and I was kind of coasting. He was making plays in the backfield. I was falling down. He was tackling the quarterbacks, who were not happy with me. They were getting hit and they were mad. Lou was sitting there on his golf cart, smoking his pipe. You could tell he was getting madder and madder. All of a sudden, that pipe and its smoke started getting closer and closer. Lou shouted, "Tim Grunhard, get your butt out now."

My backup, Winston Sandri, came running in. Lou then said, "No, get out, get out, we're playing without a right guard. You haven't blocked him all day anyway. So why would we put somebody in there? It doesn't matter. We practiced without a right guard in the first half of the practice. We might as well practice without one during the second half."

I had a tear running out of my eye; it was embarrassing. Zorich actually reveled in it. After about three or four plays, Lou said, "Get back in there."

I got down to business. I learned that day that you can't take days off. You can't take reps off. That was an unbelievable lesson that I carried over into Kansas City with the Chiefs. Every time I got out on the field, I remembered that feeling. I'm not saying I was perfect, but I promise you I never gave 20, 30, 40 percent in practice again. I never wanted that feeling again. And to Zorich's credit, I would tell him after games, "Thanks a lot, Chris."

He would say, "For what?"

"The guy I played against today was only half the player you were in practice all week. I prepared against a guy who was better than the guy I was playing against today."

We hated Lou's practices, but they certainly got us ready for games. Heading into my junior year, we weren't highly thought of. We lost a lot of veteran players from the previous season. Our offensive line had very little experience. I think I had the most starts with five. The rest of them had zero. The pollsters looked at how many veteran guys we lost and ranked us 12th in one poll and 13th in another. But we knew we had a chance to be good. We had a quarterback named Tony Rice who came into the game against LSU our sophomore year and started a little bit, but we knew that as soon as he got some snaps and got his feet underneath him, he was such a great athlete that the cream would rise to the top. Then we had a young running back by the name of Ricky Watters and we had Anthony Johnson, who was a throwback fullback. We knew that those guys were very, very talented.

The first game of the season was against No. 9 Michigan. That game was won by the smallest member of our team, Reggie Ho, who was a kicker from Hawaii. He never really played much football because he was about 5'5". He kicked four field goals that day, including the game-winner with 1:13 left in order for us to beat Michigan. It was the first night game played at Notre Dame Stadium. They actually brought in lights to light up the field. We struggled offensively, but we were able to move the ball just enough to get into field-goal range and kick field goals. Once we won that game, we had a really tough game against Michigan State at Michigan State. We won that one 20–3, and our confidence started to build. It's like anything else in sports. The Xs and Os and Jimmys and Joes are important, but it's the confidence that carries you. It's not only the confidence of the players and the confidences of the coaches making those calls, but it's also the confidence of the fans and the fanbase. That started to build.

That Michigan game also taught us the value of team. You can't rely on one player to win a game, you can't rely on one position. It depends on everybody; every single person plays a role. That's a lesson you learn as a young football player. It might be easier for an offensive lineman because you always understand that the five guys work as one. But if you're a star wide receiver or star running back, you can pretty much take over a game in high school. But you can't do that in college. When you realize that the smallest guy on the team had the biggest role in the win, you are reminded that it takes all of us. It takes all 11.

Marty Schottenheimer would always say, "Grab an oar and row." We'd laugh at that because we didn't understand. Marty would say all kinds of quirky things, but they helped.

I always say that football is a microcosm of life. You learn so many lessons in sports, especially football, because you've got to depend on and trust the guy next to you. You understand that it doesn't matter how hard you work. If the guys around you lack that same amount of effort, it's just not going to work out. That was Marty's thesis on coaching; through hard work everybody achieves more. Whether they were football snaps, reps in the weight room, running laps, or life lessons in football, you put that experience in the bank. Sometimes you have to withdraw it at a key moment. If you don't have that experience or the extra reps, you can't withdraw from the bank. You'll have insufficient funds. The good ones learn lessons through repetition in good experiences and bad and store them in the bank. Then when they get in those situations again, they are able to withdraw that information. Marty understood that. That is why we had so much success in the '90s. No loss went without a lesson. Marty was an English teacher by trade. He was a great teacher of the little things. He would say that all the time. "You've got to do the little things. Work on the six inches between your chest and your backbone."

After three more wins got us to the No. 4 spot in the polls, we hosted No. 1 Miami. The build-up for that game basically started in 1985 with the last game of Faust's career at Notre Dame. It was a bloodbath. Miami ran up the score and just took it to Notre Dame. A lot of people thought it was uncalled for that Jimmy Johnson would do that. There were hard feelings. We played them down there in 1987. It wasn't 58–7 like it was in 1985, but it wasn't close. The final score was 24–0. So there were hard feelings between the two programs.

Both teams were undefeated in 1988. Miami was coming off a national championship and feeling pretty good about itself. But we were trying to win a national championship, too.

Early in the week some Notre Dame students called Coach Johnson's office and somehow got through. They dropped this "Catholics versus Convicts" thing on Johnson. He kind of laughed it off and then hung up on them. People found out about that and decided to make a T-shirt. There was a whole ESPN *30 for 30* on the T-shirt. It was crazy. It started with one or two guys, but they had an army of people going out selling them. The Notre Dame administration was not too happy about it. I wasn't too happy about it either. I thought it was tasteless. Miami took it personally, which they should have. But it was out there so we had to back it up.

I'm a big Star Wars fan. I remember that when the Miami truck came rolling up on Friday to drop their equipment off, it felt like the Death Star was coming. I was picturing those guys coming out in those white helmets and white uniforms looking like stormtroopers. It got real very quickly. The tunnel from the locker rooms to the field was really small. Both teams came out of the locker rooms and we met in that very small tunnel to walk out onto the field. There were some words back and forth. When we got to the field, we started to stretch. They were done with their pregame routine and they ran right through the middle of our stretch line and made some comments. All hell broke loose. There was a big scuffle, which led to a big fight in the tunnel. Lou was not happy about the situation. We got in the locker room, and he was all disheveled. Somebody probably pushed him in the scuffle. He weighed 130 pounds soaking wet, so it wouldn't take much to get him disheveled.

I have never been in a locker room that was so fired up with so much adrenaline running through it. Lou understood our emotion, but he could read a room. He knew he had to get control. He called us out and said, "If I see one of you guys throwing a cheap shot, if I see one of you guys throwing a punch, if I see one of you guys embarrass this university, not only will I take your scholarship away, I will get you kicked out of this school."

The whole room sunk. All that adrenaline and hype that was being built up just left. I remember thinking to myself, *Why would he do that? Why would he take away this enthusiasm and excitement and adrenaline?* I later figured out that it was the wrong kind of adrenaline. It was the wrong kind of enthusiasm. If he wouldn't have addressed it, it could have turned into a freak show with a lot of penalties.

When those Miami teams played, they tried to take the opponents out of their games. They did that on purpose. That's the way they played. They played loose. They used cheap shots and trash talk, and that's just the way they went about it. Lou was trying to get us to focus on our preparation instead of our anger. But then he had to get us back to being fired up because the room was flat. We'd gone from the highest of highs to the lowest of lows. As he was going through his tirade, he said at the very end, "I have just one thing to ask you guys to do." We thought he was going to say, "Play smart, play the Notre Dame way."

He said, "Leave Jimmy Johnson's ass for me."

We all looked around, knowing that Johnson would kill Lou in a fight. We went crazy again, but in the right way. Lou calmed us down and then fired us back up at the end. We came out of the tunnel and had one of our best games of all time. He did such a good job reading the room. He knew we were out of control; he got us back under his control and then got us going again.

The game was back and forth the whole time. We were up, and then Miami was up. The game really came down to two calls. Miami said that Cleveland Gary didn't fumble inside the 5-yard line going in. If they had reviewed it back then, it probably wouldn't have been a fumble, so the Hurricanes were right. But the next time they scored, a wide receiver caught the ball and then dropped it before his knee hit the ground. They ruled that the ground caused the fumble, so it kind of evened itself out. People never talk about that second one; they just talk about the Gary fumble. The game came down to Johnson's decision after they scored that last touchdown—which wasn't a touchdown. Johnson, to his credit, went for two. There was no overtime in college football then, so the game probably would have ended in a tie. He reportedly said, "We always play to win."

Miami didn't get the conversion, and we won the game 31–30. It was an epic ballgame. A lot of people think it's one of the top five college football games of all time. We stayed undefeated the rest of the year, which earned us the right to play for the national championship in the Fiesta Bowl against West Virginia.

West Virginia was an independent back then. The Mountaineers certainly weren't the power that they became later. What I remember most about that game was the size of the West Virginia offensive and defensive lines. They all looked like their mascot, the Davy Crockett-looking guy. They all had big beards and they were all about 6'6" or 6'5", and it was considered the best offensive line in the country. They were really good on the defensive line, too. A couple of those guys got drafted in the NFL and played there for a long time.

Speaking of offensive lines, the trophy for the best offensive lineman in college football is named after Joe Moore, who was my offensive line coach for my junior and senior years. He challenged us. We were a bunch of baby-faced kids who wore our ties and sports jackets. We didn't have a lot of experience going into the year. Going up against the West Virginia offensive and defensive lines, we felt like it was boys versus men.

West Virginia had a great quarterback who was a Heisman Trophy finalist named Major Harris. Tony Rice was a lot like him, just not as well-known. There were a lot of comparisons in the game. They were bigger and tougher than we were, but I think the thing that helped us win that game was that we were an unbelievably seasoned team. We played the No. 1, No. 2, No. 3, and No. 9 teams that year. We played against all those teams who were really good and we were able to find a way to win. So we had a lot of confidence going into that game.

Any time you play in a national championship game—and I've heard this about the Super Bowl, too—the next thing you know, you're in the fourth quarter. You're under so much build-up because you have to wait a month to play. The game flies by. You've really got to concentrate right off the bat. I think the team that is able to use its experience and use the coaching it received has the advantage. We saw that a little bit with Super Bowl LV. Tom Brady has been there a bunch. He had a lot of confidence. The Chiefs were probably the better football team, but he had more experience, even though Patrick Mahomes is a better quarterback at this stage of their careers. A lot of times the team with more experience is the one that wins.

I don't remember anything that was spectacular in that Fiesta Bowl. It was just a good football game played by two good teams. Harris was knocked out of the game early in the contest. Even though he came back in, he was not the same. That was kind of the nail in the coffin for West Virginia. We led 23–6 at halftime and won 34–21, but it was never close in the second half.

We had a chance to go back-to-back as national champions, but we got beat 27–10 by Miami in the Orange Bowl, the site of its home stadium, during my senior year. We came into that game ranked No. 1, but things just didn't go our way.

A little more than a month later, we were back in the Orange Bowl. This time we were in the bowl game playing against Colorado, who had taken our spot as the No. 1 team in the country. That was the year before it won the national championship, but Colorado was playing for its quarterback, Sal Aunese, who passed away from cancer earlier in the year. The Buffaloes had one of those unbelievable years. They were a really good football team. Eric Bieniemy, the current Chiefs offensive coordinator, was the running back. He was kind of the juice on that team. He basically challenged the whole team on the 50-yard line by himself. He had a big personality. I didn't like him very much until I got to meet him after college. He's such a great guy.

We were up 14–6 going into the fourth quarter, but it was still a one-score game. With 11 minutes left in the fourth quarter, Lou called the offensive line over to him and said, "We're going to run the ball right down their throats. We're going to eat this clock up. We're going to go down and score a touchdown. We're going to win this game. This is it—the end of it."

We liked the plan. Whether we could execute the plan was another story. But we went in and did exactly that. It was one of those drives where it didn't matter what the situation was. Second and 6? Third and 2? It didn't matter. We got the first down. The 17-play, 82-yard drive was all runs and took up 8:55. It started on our own 18 with 10:27 left and ended with

Anthony Johnson punching it in from the 7-yard line with 1:32 left. I remember Colorado coach Bill McCartney screaming at his defense. He kept putting his hands up in the air like he was saying, "We can't stop them."

We had a wave of energy coming off the ball play after play. We weren't as tired as Colorado was. We just drove down and scored that touchdown and won the game. As an offensive lineman, that's your dream drive. That was my last drive of my senior year and my last drive at Notre Dame.

That built up my confidence going into playing for Marty Schottenheimer, who would tell us all the time, "A two-yard run in the first quarter will turn into a four-yard run in the second quarter, a six-yard run in the third quarter, and a touchdown run in the fourth quarter. You've got to have patience and you've got to believe in the plan. You've got to be in the best shape, you've got to be tough, you've got to be physical, and you've got to believe that there is a process and a plan."

It worked. We just wore people out. I learned that from that last drive of my college career. I took that and I put it in the bank. I took it here to Kansas City and was able to implement some of that stuff.

The practices before that Orange Bowl didn't go well. We were coming off that loss to Miami, and Holtz wasn't too happy. We had a little bit of senioritis in the bowl practices. Lou wasn't pleased with one of my techniques. He thought I was blocking too high. He said, "Come over here," and he proceeded to show me how he wanted me to do it. Here he was 5'6", maybe 130 pounds—this skinny guy wearing this windbreaker—and he was punching me in the chest. Then he said, "Now, you show me how to do it." At that point I got my hands inside, I got my hips underneath me, and I picked him up and basically put him over my head.

His feet were dangling in the air and kicking. The whole time he was saying, "That's the way I want you to do it. That's the way I want you to do it." I was a senior, so I wondered if I could get away with dropping him from that position. Instead, I just put him down. But that was Lou. It didn't matter if it was the first practice of your freshman year or the last practice of your senior year, he was going to do make you do it the right way. If you didn't do it his way, he was going to correct you.

Lou didn't want to heap praise on me because he must have thought it would make me soft. But behind the scenes, he went to bat for me. Following the NFL Scouting Combine in Indianapolis, Lou ran into Carl, Marty, and offensive line coach Howard Mudd. Lou jumped in a plane with those guys because they were going to Chicago for something. I didn't know it, but they were interested in drafting me. So they asked Lou to tell them about me. He said, "If he doesn't know your offense well enough to start by the second or third game, *I'll wash your car on the 50-yard line at Arrowhead Stadium.*" Now, that's not exactly what he said, but for the sake of our younger readers, we'll cut out the salty language.

Lou was the master psychologist. He knew what made me tick. He knew how to manipulate me. I was a pleaser. I always wanted to please. He never gave me the opportunity to do that. I never did anything right. Even when I did something right, I didn't get an "attaboy" or a pat on the back. That's the way my dad was. That's what made me into the man I am now. Maybe that's not the best way to go about life, always trying to search for acceptance or perfection and never being able to obtain it. But Lou knew that and he pushed my buttons—whether that was saying that everybody in the senior class was going to get drafted but me or talking about other people on the offensive line when I knew I had the best game. He didn't talk about it because he wanted me to be hungry.

I was born hungry, and Lou was really good at just putting that T-bone steak right in front of me and pulling it away. I was always reaching for it. I always felt like the dogs at the dog track. The dog is always chasing that rabbit, but he never catches it. That's the way I was with Lou and a lot of coaches that I had. They knew that I was always chasing that compliment. It was always right there. I could always just see it but never get it.

Lou had a different way of treating each player. He knew that if I finally felt satisfied or comfortable, I'd probably slack off. He knew everybody's buttons. He knew that some guys might wilt if he criticized them, so he built them up. He knew some guys had very little confidence. If they dropped the ball or missed a block, he would go and tell them it was okay, that they'd get it the next time. He knew that there were some guys who he had to keep hungry.

Lou would never cheer, at least not in front of me. He did it on my behalf but not in front of me. But somehow I knew he cared. To this day, I'll see Lou, and he will say, "What can I do for you?"

I saw him at his wife's funeral in 2020. He said, "Grunny, what can I do for you? What do you need?"

I said, "Coach, I don't need anything from you. What do you need?"

That's the way he is. When people ask, "What's it like playing for Lou Holtz? Did you enjoy playing for Lou Holtz?"

I say, "No, I did not."

But I do appreciate some of the lessons I learned from him. I've always had someone who believed in me, maybe more than I believed in myself. That person at Notre Dame was Tom Freeman. He was a senior at Notre Dame when I was a freshman. Because of injuries, he was one of the first people to ever get a fifth year at Notre Dame, which was a blessing for me during my sophomore year.

He was one of my hosts when I came for my recruiting visit. He was a Kansas City kid, which was another one of those crazy quirks that seems to follow me around in my life. He went to Rockhurst High School and was a heck of a football player. I basically backed him up when I was a freshman and a little bit of my sophomore year, and that kind of morphed into three guards who rotated. Tom loved football and the Chiefs. In fact, he was not drafted, but he signed as a free agent with the Chiefs and made it to one of the last cuts. It's another one of the fortunate twists for me because he became my financial advisor. He has done a wonderful job of helping me and taking care of my finances, which is so important because a lot of time people take advantage of athletes.

Tom always wanted to learn how to long snap. He knew that he was a pretty good offensive lineman, but he also knew that the more you could do in the NFL, the more it would help your opportunity to make the team. I was a really good long snapper. When I was a little kid, my dad told me, "Take this football and snap it until you can hit the tree 20 times in a row."

I would do it all the time. I was always outside. I was one of those kids who was rarely inside. Whatever season it was—whether it was basketball, baseball, football, even hockey—I was always outside doing something. Early in my junior year in high school, we played against Gordon Tech High School in Chicago.

We lost 2–0 because I snapped the ball over the punter's head through the endzone for a safety. At that point I thought I didn't want to do that anymore because I had just cost the team a win. But one of our coaches took a plastic football, and every day at lunch, I would have to go out and snap the ball to him. We had 20 minutes for lunch and then we had about 15 minutes to go outside. The whole school would be sitting there watching me snap because we'd be out there right in the parking lot where all the kids were. They would cheer when I snapped it well or jeer when I didn't. We did that for a whole season. I became really good at long snapping. I took a lot of pride in it. I also made a lot of tackles. I used to be an athlete before Marty beat the hell out of me.

Anyhow, Tom saw that I was a pretty good long snapper and he said, "After practice can we work together and can you show me how to long snap?"

We did that all the way through my freshman year and into my sophomore year. During training camp we'd be out there snapping after practice while Lou would sit in his golf cart, smoking his pipe. The one thing I remember about Holtz was the pipe smoke. To this day if I'm walking around and I smell pipe smoke, it just gets my adrenaline rushing because I knew the guy was close. At one point Lou sauntered over. While pushing his glasses up on his face, he said to Tom, "If Tim Grunhard could play guard as well as he can long snap, he'd be an All-American."

At that point Tom turned around and said, "Coach, he will be an All-American guard. Mark it down."

Here was this fifth-year senior sticking up for a guy who was basically backing him up and in a way trying to take his job. At that point I thought, *If Tom Freeman believes in me, then I can do this.*

I always underestimated myself. It was always part of my psyche. I did this on purpose because I could never rest on my laurels. I was always trying to reach and do something more than what was expected. When someone actually believed in me, I didn't just notice it. Tom changed my outlook of what I could and could not do.

When I got drafted by the Chiefs and moved to Kansas City, Tom was already living there. Our friendship grew and we became the best of friends. He is now in the ownership group with the Royals because he's had a lot of success in his life as a financial advisor. He has been my financial advisor for most of my playing career and all of my post-playing career. It goes back to a theory a friend of mine has. Every encounter you have with another person—whether it's a brief encounter at a toll booth, a business relationship, or a friendship—the other person will leave that encounter feeling better about themselves or feeling worse about themselves. He calls it "More a Person, Less a Person." You may say something to somebody and you don't know if it is going to affect them positively or negatively, but it can make all the difference in the world. That's one of the primary reasons I got into coaching. I realized that through many examples in my life that a word here and there, a pat on the back here or there, or a kick in the ass here and there makes all the difference.

Tom, at that point, made all the difference. He made me believe I could do it. I had a great sophomore year. My junior year was really, really good, and we won the national championship. Following my senior year, I was able to get drafted in the second round. I believe that whole process was started with that one comment from Tom.

I was kind of a hybrid offensive lineman. I played guard in college, but I didn't have the size of an NFL guard. I was also a long snapper. Could I be an NFL center? Some teams saw me as a center; some saw me as a guard. At the NFL Scouting Combine, I was able to work out for Howard Mudd. He was in charge of my group. We formed a relationship and a friendship. That's all I heard from the Chiefs. I never heard back from them after the Combine.

After the Combine the Tampa Bay Buccaneers, the Indianapolis Colts, and the Washington Redskins came to Notre Dame to check me out. Some teams offered to fly me to their facilities. The first team that flew me out to visit with its staff was the San Francisco 49ers. I met with their offensive line coach, the legendary Bobb McKittrick. The head coach was George Seifert, and their general manager was Bill Walsh. I knew Walsh because he was part of NBC's television coverage of Notre Dame football when I played there.

The 49ers offensive line was made up of guys who were all big-time first-round draft choices. I was a guy who was predicted to go in the fourth or fifth round, maybe even the sixth round. I was sitting there with Coach McKittrick when Coach Seifert cane in the room. McKittrick said, "You're our guy."

I was kind of taken aback. Then Seifert said, "We want you as a center." Their starting center, Jesse Sapolu, was getting older. So I went in and visited with everybody, took a tour, went out to dinner, did all that recruiting stuff. When I flew back home, I told Sarah, "They are going to pick me in the first round. I just can't believe it."

She wasn't really happy about it because she had moved to Chicago after graduation. We had dated since our freshman year. So my moving to San Francisco was going to be a big separation. It would have taken some effort to keep that relationship going. On draft day we were sitting at my parents' house with my mother and my dad, a couple of my cousins and neighbors, and my buddy Dan. The 49ers called right before the draft started and said, "We're going to take you in the first round. We're calling all our draft picks to make sure we have the right numbers and connections."

The first round took a long time. Guys were picked, guys who I thought were comparable to me. The 49ers' turn came up, and I didn't get a phone call. All of a sudden, the commissioner stepped up to the podium and said, "With the 25th pick of the draft, the 49ers pick Dexter Carter, wide receiver from Florida State."

I got a phone call right after from McKittrick. He said, "Listen, we fought for you. We didn't know Dexter Carter was going to be there at that point, but we're taking you in the second round, so be ready. You're going to be a 49er."

I said, "That's fine, whatever."

So about an hour and a half later, the phone rang, and it was Carl. He said, "Tim Grunhard, Carl Peterson, we just selected you with the 40th pick of the second round for Kansas City."

I said, "Okay. Great."

My family and friends said, "Who is that on the phone? You're supposed to be watching the draft."

I hung up and I said, "I just got drafted by the Kansas City Chiefs."

You could hear a pin drop.

Sarah said, "Where is Kansas City?"

I said, "I don't know. I think it is in Missouri. It could be in Kansas, but I don't know."

Sarah is a smart girl and she knew where Kansas City is. As a kid, I went down to the Lake of the Ozarks and Table Rock Lake. I knew the area. And I knew how much the people of Kansas City loved the Chiefs, but I had no idea of anything about Kansas City.

About an hour or two later, Carl called back and said, "We'll fly you up tomorrow. We want you to go to a Red Coater luncheon. We want to introduce you."

I got picked up by a guy I didn't know, but he was a Red Coater. He dropped me off at the Adams Mark Hotel across the highway from the sports complex. I knew nobody. I was sitting in the hotel. I had heard there's good Bar-B-Que in Kansas City so I called room service and I ordered ribs. Little did I know. (I now know most regions spell it barbecue, but in Kansas City, it's Bar-B-Que.)

The next day I got picked up by somebody in the organization, and Carl met me at the door. We walked through the offices. I remember looking out the windows toward the field and thinking, *This is such a cool place.*

It looked so big compared to Notre Dame, even Michigan. Most of the stadiums we played in in college didn't have upper decks. Because of its upper deck, Arrowhead looked big to me. From the point when Carl said he believed I could be one of those guys in the Ring of Honor or he wouldn't have drafted me, every time I would go into that stadium, I would look up and look at those names. I would say, "That's my goal."

I rented a place right by the stadium on Northern Avenue called Whispering Lakes. I had nothing. We had no idea where anything was. So we went to the Venture store on I-29 up near the airport about a half hour away. We thought that was the closest store. We didn't realize that the Blue Ridge Mall was about a half mile east. I immersed myself in Kansas City. That first night in the hotel was the only time I ever ate Bar-B-Que from room service. I quickly found out that there were a lot of great Bar-B-Que places in Kansas City.

The very first time I got on a radio show was with the guy who played offensive line for the St. Louis Cardinals named Conrad Dobler. I had fun with it, and at that point, the fans ate it up. I figured out quickly that if you're genuine with them, they'll buy into you. For the rest of my career, I tried to do that with fans. I learned that lesson very early. I had no idea what was going to happen. I thought the 49ers were the team I was going to, but 30 years later, I'm still in Kansas City.

God works in mysterious ways. This was the perfect place for me to not only raise a family, but also to feel welcome. Marty and Carl let me be me. And Kansas City liked me being me. I could never see myself living anywhere else. There were a couple of times in my career where I thought maybe I might get traded or even leave as a free agent. But those were just fleeting thoughts. This was always meant to be my home and will be my home. The Kansas City community embraced me and embraced my family. All my kids are Kansas Citians. They're not from Chicago or New Jersey. They're from Kansas City. They love the Royals. They love the Chiefs. They love Sporting Kansas City.

They love KU football. They even love MU football. That's the one weird thing, and it's very interesting. If you like MU, you hate KU and vice versa. Most people who root for those schools also hate K-State. K-State fans hate KU and Mizzou. I love KU basketball. I'm really into the Jayhawks, and that happened long before my son, Colin, transferred there to play football. People would tell me, "You can't do that."

I'd say, "Why not?"

That was funny to me. I just felt the connection to Kansas City. I just let myself be me and I just kind of bought in. My soul and Kansas City's soul connected. I can't explain how it happened or where it happened or why it happened, but it happened.

4

The Rebirth
of a Kingdom

THE KANSAS CITY CHIEFS HAD NOT HAD A LOT OF SUCCESS IN THE nearly 20 years before Carl Peterson and Marty Schottenheimer arrived following the 1988 season. The Chiefs had been to the playoffs one time since 1971, and that year (1986) they made it as a wild-card team and got pummeled 35–15 in the first round by the New York Jets. All the excitement of finally getting back to the playoffs disappeared almost immediately when the Chiefs went 4–11 (in the strike year) and 4–11–1 the next two years, finishing last in the division both seasons.

I don't know too much about what they went through before I got here. But I do think that there were some things that Carl and Marty really wanted to change. Marty was a Pittsburgh "steel town" guy who had grit. And I think he tried to draft that way. He drafted a guy like Percy Snow from Michigan State, who was a tough physical linebacker. He brought me in from Notre Dame, where we were known for grinding the ball out and trying to be physical at the point of attack. And he drafted Dave Szott, a guy from Penn State and a tough New Jersey kid. His point of emphasis in that draft was to find grittiness. He needed players to buy into that approach. So the vision I got from Marty was that he was trying to draft his personality. He was trying to find guys who had the same kind of attitude that he did.

I'll never forget walking into that stadium right after the draft with Carl. It was a Red Coater luncheon. The Red Coaters are a group of Kansas City-area business leaders who volunteer their time to promote the Chiefs. They were starving for something new. There was a nervous energy about this team and the direction it was going to go under this new regime. They were saying all the right things, but I could sense that there wasn't that trust yet. After what had happened in the 1970s and 1980s, people weren't sure what Marty was trying to do and if it was going to work.

I remember being at alumni dinners at Notre Dame with Lou Holtz speaking. Lou could get the crowd fired up about the future. That same kind of enthusiasm was starting to bubble up with Marty, Carl, and the guys who they would bring in. These people wanted to believe that it could happen. They were starving for a plan, and Marty had a vision.

One of the first things that we did when we went to training camp was to do the "Oklahoma drill," which is a one-on-one showdown in a narrow lane between cones reinforced by players on both sides. There was no hiding between those cones. Two guys lined up against each other with an offensive guy and a defensive guy. If it was two linemen, they'd see who could push the other guy backward. If it was a ball carrier or receiver against a defender, the offensive guy had to get through without being tackled. May the best man win. It was more than just how talented you were. It was more about how tough you were. It felt like a cage match. It felt like you were a gladiator. All the coaches and all the players would stand around you and cheer and try to get that adrenaline going.

I'll never forget going against guys like Bill Maas, Mike Bell, and Dan Saleaumua. It was a culture of toughness. We were all expected to buy into the grit and toughness of Kansas City, as well as the toughness of Marty. That was the first thing we were shown, the first thing that we did at a training camp. We did that at the end of practice every day that first year. You'd look up at the chart and see who you were going to have to go up against.

One day at the end of that Oklahoma drill, I was supposed to go against a linebacker. He was a guy who had been on the team for a couple of years. (I'm not going to mention his name.) We were supposed to be the last guys to go, but Marty stopped the drill before we had our chance. This guy called me out. I wasn't afraid to go against him, but Marty said we were done. This guy was being boisterous and a little braggadocious. He wanted it to be about how tough he was. Even though Marty said practice was over, he called me out.

So I said, "Okay, let's go."

I'll never forget this because I had a great rep. I drove him about 10 or 15 yards down the field and threw him into the crowd. The guys all went crazy. Marty kind of gave me that little smirk, and that guy was gone the next day. He was not looking for guys to draw attention to themselves. He wanted guys who would buy in. He wanted tough, physical guys who already had a lot of grit but weren't going to have a me-first attitude. It had to be about the team. That proved that he did not want a guy like that and set the tone for what we did in training camp that year.

We used to call Marty, "the man with no eyes." That was from the movie *Cool Hand Luke.* He would walk up and down the line while we were stretching. He would pull his aviator glasses on and stare at Szott, me, and all the offensive linemen. At least once a year in training camp, we would watch the movie *Cool Hand Luke,* and Morgan Woodward played the boss in the movie who was known for his silent, menacing glare behind his mirrored glasses. Marty walked up and down those lines and glared at us in the same way. He was "the man with no eyes," and we'd say "Don't mess with a man with no eyes." He brought that attitude of toughness.

Training camp wasn't like it is today. It wasn't a day at the country club. It was a six- or seven-week boot camp that rivaled those you think about with the military. We went full pads two or three times a day in the heat of Liberty, Missouri. It was the hardest thing I ever went through. That toughness that Marty wanted in his players fit the mind-set of the Midwest. Marty knew that and he knew that the people of Kansas City and the surrounding areas would fall in love with team-first players who wouldn't give less than total effort.

When I first got to Kansas City, the fans didn't quite know what to think about this new regime and the toughness that was promised. But it didn't take long to start seeing people wear red more often. Back in the 1980s, it was all about Royals blue. At first, the fans looked at us like that uncle who comes over once a week and drinks all your liquor and then takes off. You're in the same family, but there is no connection. Fans would come to a Chiefs game; the people were there, but it wasn't that important. They didn't live and die with us because it only mattered so much. They didn't know us. We just happened to play a game in their city. That's something that Carl and Marty wanted to change from the beginning.

Missouri is known as the "Show-Me State" for a reason. Chiefs fans wanted us to show what we were worth. Were we worth their hard-earned dollars? Often the money for season tickets was basically in exchange for going on a summer vacation down to the lake or even buying new shoes for their kids. A lot of people had to make choices. They were blue-collar fans. And we needed to let them know that we were just as dedicated as they were. It was our job to show them that it was worth coming out and watching this team play because we were going to play for the right reason.

The fans bought into our culture, which made it a long-term relationship that exists today. It was epitomized with our displays of toughness and a strong work ethic. Even when things didn't go perfectly, they were still fans because they knew the effort went into it. I really don't think it was just about winning. It was more about trust. Marty understood that the Chiefs needed the fanbase to trust that we would give our all, that we would work just as hard as they did to pay for that ticket.

We would show them that their hard-earned dollars would be valued, and the entertainment value was going to be there. I saw this early in my career. I learned a little bit from Mike Webster, who the Chiefs signed after he spent the first 15 years with the Pittsburgh Steelers building a Hall of Fame career. The Chiefs initially made him an offensive line coach before allowing him to return as the starting center, and he became my mentor my rookie year. Webby was an old-school, hard-nosed player who gave everything he had every play of every game. That resonated with me because I always wanted to be the guy who would represent that blue-collar fan.

That's why I always ran to the line of scrimmage when the huddle broke. That's why I always finished plays down the field. When our running back was tackled, I'd go pick him up. When our quarterback was sacked, I'd be right there to pull the defender off. I was always the first guy downfield to celebrate with my teammate when a touchdown was scored. That's why I played hurt. That's why I played sick. I never missed practice because I felt that I was representing the Chiefs fans' commitment to being there. If they were committed to be a part of this kingdom, if they were going to be committed with their hard-earned dollar, I was going to be committed to giving them the best that I possibly could.

I wasn't the only one who did that, but that's what I could personally control. And when the guys in the huddle saw me running to the line of scrimmage, peeling people off the pile, helping people up off the ground, or celebrating touchdowns, it's contagious. And that's what the fans love. They want to see that you care. If one of their buddies was in peril or one of their buddies just did something great, they'd be there for them or with them. They didn't want to see you walk back to the huddle. They didn't want to see a guy focusing the attention on himself when he scored a touchdown. It's not all about me; it's about us. It's about team. It's about community. It's about being a Kansas City Chief. It's about the community of Kansas City. We really wanted to represent that attitude.

When I first got to Kansas City, the Chiefs had just come off their first winning season in three years in 1989 when they went 8–7–1. Before that it was almost 20 years without really any success at all. The fans' interest was piqued in 1989, but it took a while for them to really invest. It was not just the fact that we were starting to win and make the playoffs. It was how we got there that they could identify with. We needed the fans to fall in love again. We needed to gain their trust and build a strong personal relationship between the players and the fans. They needed to feel like family under the guise of "one family, one kingdom." I don't think they felt that under the previous regime.

One of the things that helped with that was letting the players show their personalities. Management let the players be involved around the community, to become one with the fans. More than allowing us to do so, it was encouraged. They almost insisted that we get out there. They weren't this blunt. But unless you were someone who wanted to engage with the fans, they really didn't want you on the team.

I learned this early. I was lucky enough to do a couple events my rookie year. I talked to some of the people who were at those events, and they talked about how the Chiefs were their team again. Part of that was the marketing that the Chiefs were doing at that point. Pro football is a business, and this was a business decision. But the Chiefs knew that if the fans identified with the players, they would support them. They were way ahead of their time.

I learned a valuable lesson early in my life that this was important. I never really thought about it until I got back to the point where I had the opportunity to sign autographs and be with the people. When I was very young, maybe eight or nine years old, I was waiting in line at the mall for an hour to see Walter Payton. I was a huge Chicago Bears fan. I'll never forget the anxiousness and excitement that I was going to meet an NFL player. I got up to him, and he took my picture, signed it, and just kept going. He never looked up, never made eye contact. He never said, "Hey, thanks for coming."

It was such a disappointment. Yeah, I got to meet this player, but I just didn't feel any kind of personal connection. All I wanted from Payton—all I wanted from any NFL player—was to make eye contact and to know that he knew that I was there. I wasn't fortunate enough to be able to buy tickets to go to football games, but I never missed a game on TV. I loved the Bears. But I kind of left there losing a little bit of that innocence. I learned that some of these guys weren't exactly the kind of guys that I thought they were. Now maybe Payton had someplace to go and he wanted to sign as many autographs as possible before he left. I don't know what else was going on in his life at that time. But I never wanted that to happen to someone who wanted my autograph. Every time I did an event, I wanted to let people know that they were important. I always made eye contact. I always said, "Hey, thanks for coming." I always made sure that they understood that their time was just as important as my time.

What was so cool about Kansas City at that time was that you could go to a local grocery store, a mall, or a gas station and you could see an NFL player. I never met any other NFL players in a big city like Chicago. The Chiefs drilled that opportunity into our heads. I remember going to Venture, a local department store chain in Kansas City, and I was signing autographs. At that point, the fans were hungry for a relationship with the players. I autographed pictures, I held their babies, I shook their hands, I put my arms around people and took photos. I was like a politician.

The Chiefs understood that. It wasn't just me; it was that generation of Chiefs players. That's why people were invested. I'll never forget going to Belton, Missouri, for a Christmas tree lighting ceremony late in my rookie year. Belton is not in the heart of Kansas City. It's a small town on the outskirts of the metro area. It would have been easy to overlook Belton. But the Chiefs didn't, and I was glad to be asked to be there. People were so excited. We stood out there in the cold and drank hot chocolate. We just stood around like old friends and talked, and I signed autographs. I was with my people.

Because of events like that, the fans were personally invested in us; they were personally invested in me. Through that they became personally invested in the team. And that was our goal. Our goal was to get the fans to not only come to the games, but also to say, "I saw that guy earlier in the week signing autographs and I have a personal relationship with him. He paid attention to me."

When they would come to a game, they would root for their Chiefs player, a family member who they had met earlier in the week. I think the players cared about the fans in the '80s, but they didn't have the vehicle to carry out that compassion. Carl and Marty gave us that vehicle through radio, charity events, and being out and about and becoming a fabric of the community. People will personally invest in people that they meet. They knew us and they felt like we cared about them. When they came to the game, they came out in droves because they felt that we knew them. They were part of us. They felt in their hearts that they were all part of that big family, and that family was the Chiefs Kingdom. It's really a grassroots thing. The people were investing in the team for the individual players. And then it's the expression that "a rising tide lifts all boats."

By one guy rooting for me, his neighbor rooting for Szott, and another neighbor rooting for Marcus Allen or whoever, collectively they filled that stadium. And they started rooting for "our Chiefs." But they still had that individual connection. The thought process going around the league at that point was when you went to Kansas City, it felt like a college atmosphere. In college you go to class with these players. There's a reason the alumni feel like there's a connection. It's because they all went to the same school. The student section was always the most excited because those are their buddies out there. It wasn't just because the Chiefs fans were loud that it felt like a college atmosphere. It was a college atmosphere because people felt like they were invested in their friends. They were invested in people they knew. The front office understood that. They understood that people come out when there's a connection. Well, that was what was going on in Kansas City in the early 1990s. That connection was just getting started. It wasn't plugged in in the '80s. And that's why to this day, the people who played in the '90s, who kind of bubbled up this enthusiasm and excitement in this new thought process of bringing the family together, are some of the most popular players in the Chiefs Kingdom.

It's not because we won the most games. It's not because we were the flashiest players. It was because people knew us. People experienced us on and off the field. When I walked through the Plaza, and somebody said, "Hey, aren't you Tim Grunhard?"

I'd say, "Yeah, how are you? Thanks for coming out to the games."

There were Chiefs fans from as far back as 1963 when the team arrived from Dallas. But the 1990s was when the mantra called "Chiefs Kingdom" began. Another big reason the Kingdom exploded was tailgating. Every fanbase says they tailgate and do it right, but no one does it like Kansas City, and that was purposeful as well. Peterson not only encouraged tailgating, but he also set it up as the expectation and made it easy to do. He said, "Bring your grills and cook in the parking lot. Do what you do when you're watching from home, but do it here."

Good play on the field was just one of the keys to getting people to come to the game. An NFL game is a long event. The games are more than three hours long. When you add traffic and getting in and out and tailgating and everything else, it's an eight-hour event. There's more than four hours of other stuff. How are you going to keep people interested? How are you going to keep people motivated to come back every game? How are you going to get people lathered up for the game? Carl and Marty decided to build those four-plus hours with what Kansas City is known for. And Kansas City is known for Bar-B-Que. It was a match made in heaven. The American Royal is one of the top Bar-B-Que competitions in the country. I've heard that you can go to a different Bar-B-Que restaurant in Kansas City every day, and you won't exhaust the list in a year. Many of those restaurants started from people entered in the Bar-B-Que contests.

Almost all the great Bar-B-Que chefs in this area are also great Chiefs fans. A lot of those guys who were in the American Royal used tailgating at Arrowhead to hone their skills. That was their practice time to get their stuff going. Tailgating and the Bar-B-Que-ing became a culture. It became kind of a religion for the fans. The fans knew that they could get out there, compete, or taste the results of teams competing. They could have the best tailgate, the best setup, and the best food. Then they could go in and watch their team. That kind of built up those hours before and after the games.

I was exposed to it the first time, or when it really hit me first, prior to the *Monday Night Football* game against the Buffalo Bills in 1991. It was the first night game at home in a long time. I didn't really notice the tailgating my rookie year because I had a lot of other things on my mind. Also since it was daytime, you didn't see the smoke as much. But when I drove in for that Monday night game, that smoke was billowing over the parking lot. It was just settling over the stadium. It was rolling over the stadium like a blanket. It was like the fans were saying, "Okay, we're here to take care of our team."

That Bar-B-Que smoke became that blanket, a security blanket for me. I knew when I came in that I had those fans behind me. At that point, I would open my window. I'll never forget the smell of smoking ribs, brisket, and sausages that kind of overtook me. One thing that players always have before the game is a bit of uneasiness in their stomachs. That sweet smell of Bar-B-Que made me a little sick to my stomach. But it also exhilarated me. It was kind of like that trigger like, *I'm here. I've got to get ready for a game.*

From that point on for the rest of my career, every time I would drive into the parking lot several hours before the game, I would roll my window down and smell the smoke and the Bar-B-Que. That trigger was getting me ready for the game. It both sickened me and exhilarated me, and I was hooked. For the next nine years, my trigger to know that I was getting ready to go out there and focus on my game was to smell that smell. It didn't matter what time it was. If it was a noon game, I drove in at 8:00 AM. If it was a night game, I was getting there about 4:00 PM. The smell of Bar-B-Que really heightened my senses. It was my trigger and it was a trigger for a lot of players. And I think it was a trigger for the fans. They knew: *Okay, here we are. Let's get ourselves ready.*

It also didn't matter to the fans what time the game started. When I got there, they were already there. They got there as early as the team would let them in the parking lot. It's funny, but eventually the Chiefs had to lock the parking lot gates on Saturday night or people would have started even earlier. They couldn't wait to get in and stake their claim to a little piece of the Kingdom.

That was their pregame—just like how we went out and stretched and ran through drills. We would get all taped up and do all the superstitious stuff that we did like putting our socks on at the same time, putting our pads on at the same time, putting our shoes on at the same time every day before a game. Well, they had their superstitions too, and it was all wrapped around tailgating. Little did we know that Dr. Pavlov was one of the tailgaters. He had his Bar-B-Que grill going, which is what set us dogs off and running to beat the snot out of our opponent.

People who are part of the tailgating today could tell you where they parked for every game for the last 30 years. They can tell you what they cooked for every game, who they were with. They brought their little kids, and their little kids are now bringing their little kids, and they're still in the same spots cooking the same things. That was their game. That was their chance to go out there and show what they could do on a Sunday and then go watch their player. Tailgating was a social connection between fans. They might have each been there to root for their favorite player, somebody they had met at an event. They wore that player's jersey, but it was a Chiefs jersey, just like the fan in the next tailgate. His jersey was a different player's jersey, but it was a Chiefs jersey, too. That social connection from fan to player got them to cheer for the team. And cheer they did. Very loudly.

Communication in the NFL is the most important thing that you can have. We talked about it with the young offensive line in 2021 that had three starters on Opening Day who had never taken an NFL snap. They had to learn to communicate. If you don't communicate, you hesitate, and if you hesitate, you lose in the NFL because everybody is talented, strong, fast, and skilled.

The advantage we had in the 1990s was that we had active participation by the fans to cause penalties from people jumping offside because they couldn't hear. I've often given this example when people ask, "What's it like to play in front of 80,000 screaming fans?" It causes issues with concentration and communication.

It causes issues with hesitation. The closest thing you can do to simulate it is get in your car with all the windows closed and turn the radio as loud as it goes. Then get on I-435 in bumper-to-bumper traffic. Try to concentrate and try to manipulate your way through traffic. It's hard to concentrate. It's hard to make decisions. It's hard to see what's coming and what's not coming because the background noise is so loud that it just eats up all your senses.

That's what we had with the fanbase here in Kansas City. With Carl and Marty, being an active participant with the fans was an important factor in helping us have success. In my life I've had active participants who helped me, and that's why I loved to interact with the fans because I understood how important they were. I understood the role that they were playing. I wanted them to understand that, too. No, they couldn't go in the locker room and get dressed for the game. No, they couldn't score a touchdown or throw a key block, but their role was just as important as the role that we were playing. I can't tell you how many times Hall of Famer Howie Long would come up to me after a game and say, "That fanbase is unbelievable."

His Raiders had and have a different kind of fanbase. They were loud, but they were temperamental. Junior Seau and Cortez Kennedy had the same reaction. Kennedy even said that the Seattle Seahawks' former home in the Kingdome, which was basically a cement pie, was loud at times but nothing compared to the open-air circus called Arrowhead. Other teams would take notice. I thought that was a compliment to our fans.

Chiefs owner Lamar Hunt knew that as well and he did his best to cultivate it in his own way. He would always make it a point to walk through the crowd before the game, and Clark Hunt does it now. Lamar would go to the tailgates. He was doing his part to let people get to know him personally. The Chiefs still have a veritable parade every game day. The Chiefs Cheerleaders, KC Wolf, and the drumline all tour the parking lots, dropping in on different tailgates. The idea started at the top. It may have been Peterson's idea originally, but the Hunts bought into it right away, and it spread throughout the organization.

There's one other group that was impacted by the tailgating phenomenon. The national media took notice. The national television broadcast teams and the national print media started writing about the intimidating fans and their tailgating. When we were on *Monday Night Football* against Buffalo, there were 26 other NFL teams who were watching that game. When they heard and read about the intimidating crowd at Arrowhead, they had to think, *We've got to go to a game there later this year.*

There was an intimidation factor with the connection between the fans and the players that may not be there at other typical NFL cities. Other teams had to bus through that. When I went into other stadiums, there'd be a couple people who would be giving us "the one-finger salute." But I can't imagine what it felt like to be in a bus driving into Arrowhead Stadium and seeing 60,000 people out there tailgating with smoke billowing. The fans were setting up tents, going in and out of painted buses—all so that they could get ready for the football game. The excitement of that parking lot was the first thing that they experienced when they drove in, and I know that that was an intimidating factor for a lot of those guys.

The next thing that helped build the Kingdom was radio. Remember, we didn't have social media in the early 1990s. We had to be social offline. The best way to do that was for us to host radio shows. Players really weren't encouraged to do radio and TV events before the '90s. There were some incidents of guys who did media away from official team functions, but that was the exception. Carl took it to the next level. Once again, he knew that we needed players to build a relationship with this fanbase and to get to know them personally. That personal investment equaled financial investment. And while players around the league were starting to get involved in local media, many of them did their shows from a studio somewhere.

But if you're sitting in a bar or restaurant talking about the team and you're talking to these people like you're sitting in their living room, there's going to be a connection. That's what we really tried to do. If you're sitting around the dinner table, and there I am, maybe sitting with Joe Montana, you're going to remember that. Then, if there were six or seven other people at the table, and they were talking about how excited they were for the game, what they had to do to win that game, and how important it was to get the fans to the game, the fans could understand their role in the success of the team.

That's one of the things I would tell the fans all the time on Thursdays when I was doing my show at The Levee in Westport. I'd say, "Okay, after this radio program is over, you're not allowed to talk until Sunday because you have to save your voices. You need to be loud on Sunday." A lot of those people took it seriously.

That was their trigger. Instead of me sitting in their living room and talking to them about each game, talking about the game the previous weekend, we were doing it in a place that would allow more of them to gather. They thought they were family—and they were.

When you come back from a big-time event with your family—whether it's a wedding or whatever—you talk about how you felt, what happened, how things were going, and how you're going to go on from there. And that's what we did. We sat there and we talked about that game. And then we talked about the game ahead and we got them all excited. The fans could come up after the show and shake your hand and take your picture. Once again, I think it gets back to the fact that there wasn't social media back then. The social media of the day was radio or a TV set. Just like there is now with Twitter, Instagram, and Facebook with their hundreds of thousands of followers, we had influencers back then.

The team understood that since we were in the news. We were the original social media influencers doing those radio shows. And once again, it goes back to making eye contact and looking at people and talking to them. You can't make eye contact when you're in the studio. Fans felt like that if you were going out of your way to leave your house to go down to the Plaza, to Westport, or to a restaurant in Overland Park to do a radio show, you're invested because you're taking time out of your day to be with them.

It was always kind of a cult-like following of people who were always there. Whether things were good, bad, or indifferent, they were there. There were times when maybe there was only about 50 or 60 people at The Levee when I was doing the show. And there were also times when the people were lining up at noon to get into a 7:00 PM show. When you walked in there, it was like a concert, an event. You got them fired up, you got them riled up, and you got them ready. You kind of had that pep rally and kicked off the weekend that was coming.

You can't do that when you're sitting in a studio. You can only do that when you have that personal connection. The eyes are the connection to the soul. When we were in the stadium, it felt like there was a connection. This may be a little spiritual, but I feel their souls were connected to our souls when we were out there on the field. And that connection was built during the week on those radio shows and those events that we did. Most of the players had their own shows with their own following. We'd have fellow players on. We'd take turns appearing on each other's shows. We would talk about the previous game and the next game. It felt like you were sitting around the fire. It felt like you were sitting around the dinner table talking about football. That built the trust.

Because of that connection, there wasn't a lot of drop off even during some of the bad years when we had more losses. They knew that we were giving our best and that we needed their support. They needed us to entertain and to go out there and compete for them. They also knew that when things were going bad that we needed them. And there was that personal relationship.

Despite the significance of the radio shows, if the stands were filled only with people that came to the radio shows or even people who listened to the radio shows, that wouldn't be enough. It was those people recruiting other people to the family. Whether your radio show was on a Monday night, Tuesday night, or Thursday night, the next day at work was water cooler time.

That's why I did a radio show right from the beginning. I enjoy being with the people. I didn't want people to have the experience I had with Payton when I was a kid, when I felt kind of disenfranchised. I pledged to myself that I would never do that to somebody else. I also wanted people to enjoy the game more. The more you know, the more you enjoy—whether it's the Xs and Os or the Jimmys and Joes, whether it's what to do against a Cover-2, or why there's the pre-snap switch from a 4-3 defense to a 3-4. We'd tell them we're going to have to throw the ball more against the next opponent and we'd talk about protections. If you know more about the game, you kind of understand what's going on and you'll enjoy it more. The more you are invested, the more you understand, the more enjoyment you have.

It would have been easy for Carl to tell all the players to be engaged in the community and then sit back and watch. But he led by example. He had his own radio show. The president/CEO/general manager of the team was out there engaging with the fans. It wasn't always easy because people weren't bashful about telling him the mistakes they thought he had made. But he was willing to build that relationship, that trust, which made it easy for the concept to work all the way down to the lowly center. Peterson didn't just say: "I want you guys to do radio shows. I want you to get out in the public."

He had a title this long, but he was not afraid to get out into the community and do this himself. People didn't criticize players to our faces. *How can you let that guy get past you and sack the quarterback?* But they weren't afraid to say to the general manager, "How come you didn't get that wide receiver? How come you made a bad draft pick?" He opened himself up to criticism and to praise. That was extremely important. There were times when there were a lot more people at the players' shows than there were at the general manager's show. Let's be honest: we're competitive athletes. There was a bit of competition between us. But it fed into this trust idea that even the general manager cared enough to come out and be with us.

It was not pretty at times for us as players, and I'm sure it was tough at times for Carl. But that goes with the business. And he understood that. But he also understood how important it was for him to be out and be a part of the community and be a part of that fabric. If he was going to ask us to go out and do these things, yeah, he was also going to do that. I always gave him a lot of credit for that. The general manager is very rarely the most popular guy in an organization. But he understood that if he put himself out there and took the criticism and the praise, then the fanbase could say, "Okay, he's our guy."

That was important not only for us as players, but also for the organization. I don't know that we ever talked about it as players, but maybe it was there subconsciously. There were times when it was tough to get guys to come out for a show. Guys were tired or beat up nine or 10 games into a season. You've got to get guys after they had dinner and they're ready to kick their feet up. It wasn't easy at times.

But if management could do it, then we could do it. If the fans could show up after they finished a long day of work, we knew we'd better personally invest if they're going to financially invest in it. We wanted people to know us and to be invested in us. Because once again—and I think this is important—this is a business. It's not a fraternity or sorority. This isn't a club. This is a business. If you're personally invested, then they'll financially invest. I can't overstate the importance of these shows being on location where the fans could be. They might not have been able to afford tickets to the games, but they could afford to go to a local restaurant and grab a burger and listen to the show.

Those 50 to 100 people who came to the show led to another 50 to 100, which led to another 50 to 100. Win, lose, or draw, Chiefs Kingdom came together to celebrate every Sunday. We were all there doing it together. And if we lost, we went onto the next week. If we won, we celebrated. We always had each other; we always knew that the fans and the players were connected. And they were connected through the events.

Let's be honest: the radio shows are another good example of ego building. For the most part, people didn't come to the shows or listen to the shows to boo us. We were the celebrities who people wanted to see, and it certainly was an ego stroke. I had my following on Thursday nights. Neil Smith and Derrick Thomas had their following on whatever nights they did their shows, so we each had our pockets of people. The one common thing you all had was Sunday, where all of those pockets came together and filled Arrowhead Stadium and rooted for us as a group.

But Carl and Marty knew that for the Kingdom to grow, we had to invest more than just a weeknight in a bar or restaurant. They encouraged us to establish foundations for charity. For example, I got involved early on with First Downs for Down Syndrome. We all poured our own time and many times our own resources into these organizations that have benefited others, which fits the Kansas City mentality. Anybody who walked into Arrowhead Stadium throughout the '90s noticed that the place was painted with signs of guys' charitable works. Whether it was Derrick's Third & Long Foundation, Neil's Sack Club, or Dan Saleaumua's charity, everybody had a foundation. Along the walls were all those posters and banners. To us, that was really important to share and give back.

When TV sports reporter Gordon Ducking asked me to be a part of First Downs for Down Syndrome, it hit home. I had two cousins with Down syndrome. It was just a natural fit for me to lend my time for that initiative. It made us feel good that we're giving back to the community, making a difference in some people's lives, and raising money so that charities could do special things. But it also sent a message to the fanbase that that we were invested in Kansas City, that we were a part of the fabric of the community. And through charitable works, we were able to show that.

I can't tell you how many players that I played against would walk off the field after games and say, "Man, this is so cool. You guys do so much around the community. You know, I wish we had something like that with my team and community."

That's what was special about Kansas City. Not only were we a part of the community, and they were a part of us, but we also tried to take the less fortunate, who really needed our help, and boost their lives. We represented the people who had special needs or special problems, which prevented them from coming to games, through our foundations and charities on the field. So we carried a little bit of that organization with us.

All of these things that Carl and Marty encouraged fit me to a tee. I couldn't have been drafted by a better team because the culture they were trying to build fit me perfectly. When you go through the draft process, the teams call your college head coach, your position coach, even the high school coach to find out what type of player you are. Maybe the Chiefs were looking for someone who cared about the fans. Maybe they wanted somebody they knew was going to be outgoing and be a part of the community. And it all really bounces back that I had that experience when I was a young kid. I didn't feel like I was part of the Chicago Bears family. I held that in the back of my mind with everything I did from that point on.

I'm not saying it was a life-changing event because I always cared about people. But the one thing that I wanted to do was to share my excitement and my enthusiasm. I love the game of football. And in my experiences with the fans, they knew that I cared about them and they were a part of the family. And they knew that I was out there doing the best I could, playing through injury, playing through different problems, and not missing a beat. They knew that I was invested in them as much as they were invested in me.

That was kind of the springboard for what happened. It was not just me. I was a part of it, but there were other people, too. But that was what built the foundation. The "center" of that foundation was built on trust, love, and commitment. I love the fans of Kansas City. I needed them to trust me and I needed to be committed to them. When I was out and about and I met somebody, I was going to look him in the eye and say hello. I was going to shake their hand and make them feel like they were important. I was going to make them feel like they made a difference. I was going to let them know that their love and their excitement for the Kansas City Chiefs and for me was right back at them.

5
My Teammates

IN MY 11-YEAR CAREER WITH THE KANSAS CITY CHIEFS, I PLAYED with approximately 500 different players. Sometimes we were teammates for just one year; others were for a lot longer. Some of my teammates made just a small impact on my life; others changed my pro football career and life. However, there's no way I can rank the impact that these 14 guys made on me and on my career. So I'm going to chicken out and list them alphabetically. (Meet me at The Levee sometime, and I'll give you my rankings.)

Marcus Allen

I didn't like Marcus Allen the first time I met him. It wasn't anything he did. It was totally me. I went in thinking about Marcus Allen as a USC Trojan and a Raider—two teams I was programmed to hate at Notre Dame and with the Kansas City Chiefs. But I was totally wrong. Marcus was a pro. A pro is the biggest compliment you could give another professional athlete in any sport. I never met another player who respected the sport more and had more attention to detail than Marcus.

He was a gifted athlete, like most Hall of Fame players, but he understood and taught me to learn the game in every aspect, every detail. That is what separated him from being good to

102 ◆ View from the Center

great. Marcus would go into the offensive line room after practice. We'd be meeting, watching practice or game film as a unit, and he would ask us what we saw in different situations. He would ask about our communication in different situations. Then he would store the information in his mental toolbox and take it out on the field.

We called him "Cutty" because his vision was almost super-human. He would see defenders move before they would do it. And he based his movements off of instinct. His instinct was heightened because he was the best prepared football player on the field.

The best $20,000 I ever spent was to pay a fine for a fight that I got into to save Marcus. We were playing against the Seattle Seahawks in the mid-1990s. Marcus was pushed into the Seahawks' bench at Arrowhead Stadium. When I saw that, I scurried over there to try to help him up. When I got there, I realized that Marcus, who had been pushed underneath the opposing bench, had come out swinging. At that point, I went in full barrel and helped Marcus get out. I may have thrown a punch or two. That cost me $20,000. But Marcus respected me more than ever, and it was the best $20,000 I ever spent.

Marcus would come on my radio show every year at Christmas time, usually with his yellow lab named Bess. It was a tradition that we did every year when he was a Chief. We would talk about football, talk about the previous game, and talk about the game to come. But that show was the highlight of the year because of the last segment. We finished the show singing Christmas songs together with the crowd.

It was important to make a connection to let our fans know that we were a big family. That was accomplished during this particular show every year. The smiles, the tears, and the oneness that was gained during "Jingle Bells" and "Santa Claus Is Coming to Town" was undeniably the best chance for Marcus to let his hair down through a song with his fans. He was a Hall of Famer in every right—other than his singing voice. He could not sing. Neither could I, but we really thought we were good. There's a *Kansas City Christmas* album that came out in the mid-1990s. They taped one of the times we sang "Santa Claus Is Coming to Town" and put it on that album.

The very first time he came on was right around Christmas in his first season. And at the end of the show, we just kind of started singing Christmas carols. I don't totally know how it came to be, but it was just the last segment, and we thought, *Hey, let's sing. Let's get the crowd into this.*

Well, that became a tradition. The next three or four years that he was in Kansas City, we would actually print out all the words for the crowd and we would plan that the last 20 minutes of the show was going to be the Christmas carol time. People knew it was coming, and they loved it. They would dress in their Santa Claus outfits. And they would be ready to sing along. Marcus loved it because it let him bond with the crowd probably differently than he ever could have done in Oakland or L.A. He really loved Christmas. He was one of those guys who decorated his locker. He was just a little kid at heart.

As I look back at it, Marcus and I were an odd couple. There was the Notre Dame versus USC thing. He was a former Raider. He was from L.A., and I was from Chicago. But the idea of singing Christmas carols in front of a live audience embodies what Carl Peterson and Marty Schottenheimer wanted us to do. We were just a couple of normal guys and we let the people see that. We just happened to be better at football than they were.

The best moment I had with Marcus was in a road playoff game against the Houston Oilers. It was toward the end of the fourth quarter, and we were up by a point while deep in Houston territory. A touchdown would ice the victory. As I stood in the huddle, Marcus walked in, and I said, "Marcus, I'm just a fat kid from Chicago playing offensive line. You need to get this in the end zone."

He said "All right, Grunny, I gotcha."

Marcus scored the touchdown and even mentioned in his book that he "went out there and scored that last one for Grunny."

John Alt

John Alt was kind of like Paul Bunyan, the guy with the big blue ox named Babe. He was a humungous man who was about nothing but playing football, hunting, and fishing. That's all he liked to do. Being a guy from Minnesota, one of his favorite things to do was ice fish. In the winter you would find this hunk of a man sitting on ice with the temperature probably about 10 below zero, waiting for his flag to tip. And he loved that.

John was very quiet, very reserved, but as far as energy, he was Superman. He did his best work in the cold, icy weather. The colder it got in Kansas City, the more energy he had. One year, we were playing against the Broncos in Denver. Early in that game, it was just misting. There was a forecast that said that we might get a little bit of snow during the game, but it was probably only 40 or 50 degrees. As the game went on, it got a little bit colder, and a couple of flakes started to fly as we went into halftime. Coming out onto the field after halftime, there was three inches of snow on the ground, which I guess can happen in Denver.

That was awesome for us because one thing offensive line-man love is snow. We love it because it slows the defensive linemen down. As offensive linemen we know where we're going. Defensive linemen have to react. And the reaction times fall off when you have snow or cold or rain. As the game went on, we noticed that John was getting more talkative. He was getting more energized. And he was just dominating. I can't remember exactly who he was playing against. But he was just destroying the guy in front of him. John never said much, especially in the huddle. But as snow was piling up on his shoulder pads and on his helmet, he just looked at us and said, "I'm strong now" and ran to the line of scrimmage. He finished that game pancaking everybody in sight. That's my fondest memory of John.

Keith Cash

I don't think that you can talk about the Kansas City Chiefs in the 1990s unless you talk about "the spike," when Keith Cash threw the football against a poster of Buddy Ryan's face in the end zone. Let's rewind it to earlier in the year.

We were playing against the Houston Oilers, and Joe Montana was out. John Alt was out. I think Dave Szott was out. I think Joe Valerio was starting next to me. I can't even remember who was playing tackle, maybe Danny Villa. The offensive line was just in shambles. It was a little bit like Super Bowl LV for the Chiefs, when all five starters were injured. It was bad.

The Oilers were blitzing us and they were running that 46 defense. They were a good defense anyway, but with a depleted line, we couldn't pick anything up. We were shut out 30–0. It was a disaster and an embarrassment. We were embarrassed by Buddy Ryan, who stood on the sideline with his arms crossed and a little smirk on his face. He was enjoying the whole process of embarrassing us and embarrassing Marty Schottenheimer. Paul Hackett was the offensive coordinator, and Ryan enjoyed embarrassing him. We kind of took that personally.

All week leading up to the playoff game, we talked about wiping that smirk off of Ryan's face. That was our rallying cry. We wanted to win a playoff game on the road, something the franchise hadn't done since 1969. But as an offense, we wanted to knock the smirk off Ryan's face.

As the game started, it was a little bit of the same thing. The Oilers were blitzing, and we just couldn't get anything going. But right before the half, we had an incomplete pass. You would think that wouldn't be a good thing. But it was the telltale sign that we could do this. We picked up their blitz. Willie Davis beat their corner deep, and Joe Montana just overthrew it; it was off the tip of Davis' fingers. But we knew at that point that we could pick up the blitz. It took six quarters to figure out what Ryan was trying to do to us, but we finally figured it out. We went into the locker room down 10–0, and Keith and the other receivers and tight ends were saying, "We're gonna knock the smirk off Buddy Ryan's face."

Early in the third quarter, Keith caught the ball. Usually, he didn't score a lot of touchdowns. He was basically another option if all the receivers and backs were covered. But he caught the ball in the flat and cruised in to score a touchdown. All in one motion, he took the ball and fired it at the poster just a few feet away, as if to knock the smirk off Ryan's face. I'm sure Ryan would say that was uncalled for. But he was pimping us about his defense. That was a ceremonial "knock the smirk off."

Whenever I go to an event, somebody always comes up to me and says, "We remember when Keith Cash threw that football at Buddy Ryan's face."

That was kind of an iconic moment of the '90s. Keith was the one who did it, and I couldn't think of a better guy to do it.

Steve DeBerg

The first time I met Steve DeBerg was an indication of my relationship with him for the next couple of years that we played together. It was May 1990, and I was sitting at my locker getting ready to go out on the field for my first minicamp. I was scared to death.

It was time to "practice with the varsity team." Those guys looked like men, and I still felt like a little kid from the south side of Chicago. It was then that my offensive line coach, Howard Mudd, walked up to me spinning a football in his hand and said, "Grunny, we're going to put you at center."

That was totally foreign to me. I was forced into action one game my sophomore year at Notre Dame when we played at Michigan, but other than that, I never played center in my life. I looked at him and said, "Yes, Coach, whatever you want."

He handed me the ball that he was spinning and said, "Go over there and have Bergie take some snaps from you."

And then he walked away. I didn't have the guts to ask him, "Who's Bergie?"

I asked the only person I kind of knew, Jonathan Hayes, whose brother coached me in college. Hayes dismissed me and said, "The guy across the locker room laying on the floor."

I thought, *That old guy is our quarterback?*

So I walked over. Not wanting to call him Bergie yet, I said, "Mr. DeBerg, Howard wants me to snap a couple to you before we go out."

Steve was kind enough not to say anything, but the sounds of old bones creaking told the story: he was none too happy about having to get up for some rookie he didn't even know.

I remember thinking, *I'd better get used to this odd feeling of hands, well, you know where.* My snap made a nice, crisp sound, and Steve said in his beach boy brogue, "You got it. I'll see you out there." Then he laid back down.

Nothing ever riled him up or got his attitude in a bunch, which established our relationship in the huddle for all those years with the Kansas City Chiefs. Bergie never met a beer he didn't like. He was a life of the party—whether it was in his home in Lakewood, Missouri, or the parking lot at Arrowhead.

He showed the youngers guys—and just about everybody on the team was younger than Steve—that you play hard and party hard. I'll never forget the time we went to Dodgertown in Vero Beach, Florida, for a playoff game practice against the Miami Dolphins. That's when I was first introduced to "aisle surfing." As the plane took off, he grabbed the blanket from the overhead and surfed the aisle all the way from first class to the coach bathrooms. He was crazy.

Even to this day, Bergie lives life to the fullest. His magician-like ball handling on the field was legendary. But his drinking from the chalice of life was just as impressive. He was the perfect quarterback to set the tone for the attitude of the 1990s: play hard, work hard, enjoy the game, and share your zeal with the fans.

My favorite moment was after a game we played against the Seattle Seahawks. Both Steve and I got hurt in that game. I tore my left thumb ligament, and he broke his left (non-throwing) pinky finger. I think he was following through and hit his hand on a defender's helmet. He had an early-week operation. His finger was sideways, not the way it was supposed to go. He looked at it and was pretty nonchalant about it. We were all like, *Holy crap.*

The next week, when we came on the field, I had a big cast on my hand, and he had some odd-looking Erector Set pin coming out of his finger. Like the first time we met, we were asked by the coaches go take a snap together. He did something I never experienced before or since. He took a one-handed snap. That, by the way, is virtually impossible. But I heard the same crisp pop of the snap. We went on our way and played that week mostly in the shotgun.

At one point, I felt the uncomfortable feeling of a center/ quarterback exchange, but this time it was just with one hand. The play went off, and we got back to the huddle. And he said to me once again in his Cali accent, "You got it, bro. We're all good."

Bergie just loved life. He didn't care what people thought of him. He wasn't mean. He wasn't being directive, but he was going to be this surfer guy playing quarterback. And the way he handled life was a perfect transition for the Chiefs from the 1980s to the 1990s.

If it would have been Joe Montana to start out the 1990s, it might have been different. If it was Rich Gannon, it might have been different. But here was this veteran guy who had seen everything and done everything. He was the veteran quarterback who held down the starting position while the San Francisco 49ers got Montana ready. He did the same thing for the Denver Broncos and John Elway and for the Tampa Bay Buccaneers and Vinny Testaverde. Nothing fazed him. The young guys learned from him. This was before any of us had radio shows. But Steve's attitude kind of gave us the green light to be engaging with the fans. He didn't hide from the fans. He embraced them.

Rich Gannon

Please don't ask me to rehash who should have started the 1997 playoff game versus the Denver Broncos. Much has already been said about it. Unfortunately, I did not get a vote in the decision. Marty Schottenheimer had a rule—and Coach never broke his own rules. Marty's rule was that you would never lose your job because of injury. When Elvis Grbac was healthy, he was going to play.

I was a leader on that team. And if I would have not backed the guy who was going to start—Grbac—it would have been a disaster. But Rich Gannon was hot, and Rich would have won that game. But that's a whole different story. The story I want to talk about is Rich, the most unselfish player I've ever played with.

Rich came to the Kansas City Chiefs after battling back from a major shoulder injury. I wasn't quite sure what we were getting. We showed up in River Falls, Wisconsin, for training camp, and I soon learned that Rich was the ultimate competitor. If you were playing checkers with Rich, he'd want to tear your heart out to win. That's the attitude he had in the huddle. When he came into any game, he would do anything to get that first down. It didn't matter if he had to sit in the pocket to let a receiver clear a zone, often taking a hit because of the time needed. He would do that. The quarterbacks weren't protected like these guys are nowadays. Rich would dive headfirst to make a first down at the sticks. He would do whatever it took to win.

I'll never forget the presence he had in the huddle. That's our office on the field, and like most offices, everybody wants to talk or to complain about something. It can be hectic. Some quarterbacks can handle it, and others can't. Rich could. I learned early in my time with Rich that when he came into the huddle you shut up. I'm a pretty outgoing guy, and that carried over into the huddle at times, which would have nothing to do with speaking while he spoke or complaining about play calls. But once I said something like, "We need to run the ball."

Every offensive lineman, dating back to the time Knute Rockne developed the first forward passes, has bitched about not running the ball enough. Rich set me straight with something to the tune of: "If you want to sit back here and get your head taken off, have at it. But if not, shut up and do your job." And guess what? I did.

Of all the guys that I had on my radio show, Rich was the smartest and most genuine. That's one of the reasons he does such a great job as a color commentator every Sunday. Yes, he can relate to the fans. He can look them in the eyes and explain the game with a twinkle in that eye, so that when they walk away, they know the game a little better. Rich always wore a corny black leather jacket and painted on jeans. So he was, as you can imagine, very popular with the lady fans in the lobby. The female population would more than double when Rich was a guest on the show. The lines would be out the door.

He really didn't start many games in Kansas City. Later, he went on to lead the Oakland Raiders to the Super Bowl. I can't forgive him for that because as a Raider he shared our secrets with Jon Gruden and his new team. Raiders Week was treated special. Raiders Week was treated differently in Kansas City because of Marty. He was all about tradition. He would have posters up all over the complex. He would have daily pep talks and convince us all that Raiders owner Al Davis didn't respect Kansas City, didn't respect the Chiefs, and didn't respect Lamar Hunt. Rich told Gruden this, and they started to practice some of the same things and they beat us in 1999 and 2000. And that's something they barely ever did in the 1990s. Rich was competitive to the end.

My favorite moment with Rich wasn't even with him as a teammate. It was my first Pro Bowl, and I believe it was his as well. Our families traveled to Hawaii together, and Rich struck up a friendship and a bond with my son, CJ, who was just a toddler at the time. He threw him around in the pool. He played catch with him on the practice field. And before the game, he took him to some of the festivities. This left an impression on CJ and on me, too. The next year for Christmas, Santa brought a Raiders No. 12 jersey to a Chiefs player's house. Needless to say, CJ and that jersey went everywhere around Kansas City together, which got us plenty of strange looks and left me with a lot of explaining to do. But CJ didn't care. That's how much we respected Rich, a guy who understood what it was like to be a great teammate.

Nick Lowery

Nick Lowery was a character. When you talk about characters on the Kansas City Chiefs in the 1990s, Nick is in the top five. He was very flamboyant. He always had a pretty girl on his arm. He was always dressed to the nines, always wearing jewelry. He wore product in his hair. He was a businessman who played football. And he let everybody know that playing football was what he did—not who he was.

Nick was very conscious of everything he did as far as kicking, pregame rituals, etc. He was very particular with the way he did it. You really didn't want to get in his way because he was a kicker, and they're a little flaky anyway. Everybody kind of avoided him, especially on gameday. Nick made a lot of big field goals for the Chiefs. He's in the Ring of Honor. People seem to remember the ones kickers miss, but he made a lot of field goals that won a lot of football games for the Chiefs.

I remember preparation when we were going to play against the Buffalo Bills in a playoff game, following the 1991 season. It wasn't the AFC Championship Game, which was two years later. We noticed when we were watching the special teams film that opposing kickers were getting pelted with snowballs from the Buffalo fans. Any time a kicker was getting ready to kick, it was just like in a basketball game, when fans wave their hands behind the basket. But instead they thought the best way to get the kicker off of his game was to a throw snowballs at him.

So Marty Schottenheimer decided to get Nick ready for this. He had us tape up about 100 balls of socks. When Nick got ready to kick a field goal in practice, Marty had us throw snowballs (or sockballs) at him like the fans. Nick didn't like that at all and he started to get upset. The last thing you ever want to do is show weakness in a locker room or on a football field. Because once you show that weakness, you know it's not going to end. You've got to find a way to not show it—even if you're upset. Because if you show it, more is coming at you. But Nick was upset, and he was yelling at Marty and yelling at the guys. Marty just said, "Hey, this is what's gonna happen in the game. You got to be ready."

At one point Dan Saleaumua threw a sockball and hit Nick right in his face. Nick just had that one bar across the facemask, so the sockball went through pretty cleanly. Nick started to chase Dan around. Dan could smash Nick with one fist or crack him in half with his hands. But he was running around like a little kid, laughing and giggling. The whole team was dying as Nick was chasing Dan around. I just wish that Nick would have caught Dan so we could have seen what would have happened.

Away from competition, Nick was a pleasant guy. He was just different than we were. We were kind of these scruffy football macho guys, and Nick was the well-dressed, well-coiffed business-man. Nick is just a genuinely nice person, but he's quirky. And when you're quirky in an NFL locker room, people are coming after you.

Bill Maas

Bill Maas was the toughest, nastiest, born-to-be-a-defensive-nose-tackle guy that I've ever been around. But Billy Bob also has the biggest heart. If he liked you, he was as loyal as anybody I ever knew. He would stand up for you and he would take shots for you. Bill was a veteran when I was a rookie and he had to break me in. That was his job.

I don't know if Marty Schottenheimer told him to do it. I don't know if defensive coordinator Bill Cowher told him to do it. He just did it. It's legendary how he basically destroyed Brad Budde, Ed Budde's son. Ed and Bill are really good friends. But Brad came in and showed weakness. If Maas smelled blood in the water, he was a shark and he attacked. And he basically ran Brad Budde out of Kansas City.

I knew that when I got drafted by the Kansas City Chiefs. Jay Hayes, one of my coaches at Notre Dame, was the brother of Jonathan Hayes. Jay came to me and said, "You're going to have to deal with Billy Bob."

I said, "What's a Billy Bob?"

Jay said, "He's going to test you and he's going to make your life miserable. He's going to be rough on you. He's gonna do everything to get you off your game. So you better be ready for Billy Bob."

The very first practice we did the Oklahoma drill, and Bill and I went up against each other. I got the best of him in that drill because that was what we did regularly at Notre Dame. We ran the ball, and my role was to push the defender back. That's why I got drafted. Bill did not like that at all. So the very next time we had a team period, he hit me right across the face. And then we started to fight. I think he broke his finger on my face. I mean, that's how hard he hit me. I mean, he really laid into me. I was like, *Oh my gosh, this is going to be what I have to deal with all year, maybe the next couple years.*

The rest of team stopped to watch because they knew what Bill was doing. He was testing me. I guess I passed the test because after the practice was over I was walking up this big hill from the locker room to the cafeteria. All of a sudden, this pickup truck comes screeching around the corner and slams on its brakes. A voice said, "Get in!"

I looked in and saw Bill. I was thinking I was going to end up in the Missouri River.

He said, "You know what? I like you, kid. You're with me."

Bill had this secret entrance to the cafeteria. And at lunchtime all anybody wanted to do was to get to lunch, get back to the dorm room, and take a nap before the next practice. This is when we really practiced two-a-days. Nowadays, these kids have a walk-through practice. They may have a challenging practice every once in a while. But back in the early '90s, that second practice was always the hardest. So everybody wanted to get a little break. The key was to get in the lunch line as fast as you could. If you were a rookie, you'd be in the back of the line. By the time you ate, you'd have maybe an hour or less for a break.

But Bill took me through his back door, and we walked through the kitchen. All the cafeteria ladies and the other people that were working in there just said, "Hey, Billy, what's going on?"

They were used to him being there, and he took me along. We went in, sat down, and started eating lunch. Then the doors opened. All the rest of the guys came in, and they were all screaming at Bill. They were upset because they knew what he did.

From that point on, Bill took me under his wing. I was at his house for Thanksgivings. I went fishing with him in Canada. I borrowed his tractor to cut the grass when I bought my ranch as a rookie.

Bill was going to test you and was going to make sure that you had that toughness in order to play in this league. But once he found out that you could pass that test, he was the biggest and most loyal person I've ever been around. He was like an M&M. He had that hard candy shell, but inside it's pure sweetness.

Joe Montana

The G.O.A.T. entered the building. Joe Montana had been a legend in my eyes since January 1, 1979, the famous "chicken soup" game when Notre Dame beat Houston in the Cotton Bowl. Montana had the flu, and with the temperature in the mid-20s and a strong wind blowing, his body temperature plummeted to 96 degrees toward the end of the first half. That coincided with the Notre Dame offensive production plummeting. Notre Dame

started out clicking on all cylinders and built a 12–0 lead. But as
Montana's tank ran on empty, the team's production dropped.
Houston scored 34 unanswered points and led 34–12 heading
into the fourth quarter. Montana was sick for most of the second
half. Notre Dame blocked a punt for a touchdown at the beginning of the fourth quarter. Montana threw a pass for the two-
point conversion. That's when the chicken soup fueled him up
to lead two touchdown drives. The second one was right at the
end of the game to win 35–34. My dad said, "Now that's a leader."

My brother, Dan, and I took a football out into the backyard and we replayed the last drive in a cold alley. Fast-forward
14 years later, and Joe walked into the locker room and became
a teammate of mine.

That was the first time I met Montana, and I was starstruck.
I have to admit it. I didn't even know how to talk to him. I was
frozen. This was Joe Montana. But Joe made it easy. He said,
"Hey, Grunny, you're my center, right?"

I think I said "Yes," but who knows?

He said, "Let's go grab a bite to eat."

Of course, I jumped at the chance to hang out with Joe. The
equipment manager, Allen Wright, drove, and I sat quietly in
the back seat.

Joe said, "Hey, guys, let's go grab a beer."

There was a place in Westport called Kelly's. It was a
Wednesday night so it probably wouldn't be crowded. So off
we went.

We talked about Kansas City, like where to play golf in
town, and kind of lost track of time. Word had gotten out that
Montana was there, and the scene at Kelly's turned from a quiet
Wednesday night to something like a St. Patty's Day gathering.
The place went nuts. People were lined up out the door. Police

had to set up a blockade. Wright said we had to get out of there. That's when for the first time I saw the cult following that my quarterback had. People grabbed him. They grabbed his empty beer bottles and put them in plastic bags. One time a kid hid under his car in training camp waiting to jump out to get his autograph. Joe handled it with grace and composure. But I kind of felt sorry for him. Once you're a superstar athlete, just like being a movie star, your life is never the same.

We didn't go home after Kelly's, but we found a couple of hidden dives to escape to. I should preface this by saying that this was not planned. I had called Sarah from the locker room at 6:00 PM and said, "Joe Montana asked me to dinner."

She was just as excited for me as I was. Sarah had a picture of Joe in her high school locker. Well, the shine wore off when I got home a little after 4:00 AM. Sarah had called the hospitals and some of my buddies to see if I was okay. She thought I was dead. I said, "You don't tell Joe Montana that you're going to go home."

She looked at me and said, "Get your ass to bed. You have practice in a couple hours."

I rolled into the team meeting the next morning, and there was my new quarterback sitting in the front row looking like a CEO with a fresh shave. I had even more respect for the G.O.A.T. from that point on.

Joe went out of his way to come to at least one radio show per year. Those shows were the place to be in Kansas City. He had to come in with police escorts. Joe didn't really like being out in crowded spaces, but he seemed to understand that this was special. This was for the Kansas City Chiefs fans. I'm glad I got a glimpse into his life that he really never opened, but he did for my show. I think we even got him to say something about how he wanted to kick the San Francisco 49ers and show a certain quarterback that he was still the sheriff in the league. People in Kansas City ate it up. We opened the show with a song that was played when he was first coming to Kansas City to make his decision. He loved it.

I've talked about being disappointed when I met my hero, Walter Payton, and not feeling loved. I wanted to see if this guy was different. I wanted to see if this guy got it. Joe did. He looked people in the eye. He conversed as much as he could. But more importantly, he let people in for even just a moment. He gave them a glimpse of what it takes to be great.

We all know the stories of the greatness of Joe Montana as a Chief. They are legendary. Books have been written about such acts. But there's a story that exemplifies Joe's time in Kansas City. It was a Saturday afternoon, the day before a big home game. Joe was sitting on his couch watching college football, and the doorbell rang. He yelled for someone to get it, but nobody answered. It rang again and again. Joe couldn't take it anymore. He stepped toward the front door and looked outside. There were about 20 kids standing anxiously at his front stoop. He thought, *I really don't feel like signing anything. And I really don't have any memorabilia to give out.*

We've all looked out our front door and said, "What do they want? I'm just not feeling it."

But Joe answered the door. One of the kids said, "Hey, Mr. Montana, can your boys come out and play?"

They weren't looking for the superstar quarterback after all. I think that's one of the reasons Joe liked Kansas City. This city allowed him to be himself. He fit in so well in Kansas City. I've heard a story about when Johnny Unitas signed his biggest contract with the Baltimore Colts. He was able to buy a new house in a new neighborhood. When the neighborhood kids found out that Unitas and his family had moved into the neighborhood, they came to his door to ask for his autograph. This happened with regularity. His kids, who knew Unitas simply as "Dad," thought it must be some neighborhood tradition. So they went around the neighborhood and asked all the other dads for their autographs. The fans of Kansas City treated Joe like any other dad. They certainly recognized his talent, but for the most part, they let him live a normal life.

Joe had a great sense of humor. He was a bit of a cut-up, but he disguised it well. During one of our very first team meetings, all of a sudden, there was this horrible sulfur smell. Joe had put a stink bomb underneath his chair to get the meeting to end. People had no idea who did it. Marty Schottenheimer was not too happy about it, but it was Joe. What was Marty going to do?

When guys were in the bathroom stalls, he'd take the talcum powder and shoot it over the top on top of you. The next thing you knew, you had talcum powder all over you. Another thing he would do, especially with the centers, was slap you "underneath." Some guys will poke you to let you know the quarterback was getting down there. But he would slap you, usually fairly hard, which was not very comfortable to say the least.

But he also took care of his linemen. I'll never forget one year when we were in River Falls, Wisconsin, for training camp. Joe went to our equipment manager, Darren Kearns, and said, "I want a pizza and a six pack. I want it at their door every night after meetings." We'd come back after meetings, and there'd be a large pizza and six pack of beer, Gatorade, or Coke.

He was a trickster, but he really loved his teammates. I always felt sorry for him because he really couldn't show that. But I think he carried it over with his jokes and his little things he would do. He was one of the guys. Every time I see Joe, we kind of reminisce. He talks about how much he loved Kansas City and how he really wishes he could have stayed in Kansas City. His kids absolutely loved it.

Dan Saleaumua

Dan Saleaumua is my brother-in-law. I've already told you that I don't have a sister, and Saleaumua is not Sarah's brother, but he's still my brother-in-law. He's another guy who played defensive line early in my career, but he was the opposite of Bill Maas; he would try to make you his buddy so you wouldn't go as hard in practice against him. He naturally did not like to practice. He wasn't as bad as Derrick Thomas when it came to loafing, but he would just kind of go through the motions. If he could get away with it, he would do the least amount possible during the week in order to be ready for the game.

I didn't understand that kind of attitude. I came from a place where if you didn't practice hard, the coach would pull you. I was used to going full speed in practice. For some reason, Dan had his locker right next to mine in training camp my rookie year. He kept talking to me: "Hey, man, you make me look good during my drills, and I'll make you look good during your drills. That way, we'll both make the team."

How do you answer that? Do I say yes? Am I getting set up? Guys will set you up. They'll do anything to make the team. I figured this guy was trying to set me up. So we got to practice, and during an offensive period, I have to look good. Dan looked at me and started moving his head to one direction. I wondered what he was doing. The snap went off, and he shot that way. The very next play, we get back up to line of scrimmage, and he started nodding his head the other way. I may be dumb, but I'm not stupid. I realized that he was telling me where he was going. I said to myself, *Okay, well, I'm going to have to trust this guy. It's like the old saying*: "Fool me once, shame on you; fool me twice, shame on me."

For the rest of the offensive period, I shot across the line. I got my head across, got my hands inside, and I was driving him. Howard Mudd and Marty Schottenheimer took notice. "That's a great block, Grunhard! That's the way to get your head across. That's awesome!"

Dan said, "See, see, see, I told you, I told you." He continued to do this. And I continued to have a lot of success early in practice and in training camp against Dan.

Then we got to the defensive period. I was thinking, *What do I do here?* If he was setting me up, I could do a lot of damage to my chances of making the team. He said, "Don't worry. I'm not going to make you look bad. But I gotta get to where I need to go."

This was all going on at the line of scrimmage. I finally figured out how to tell him where I was going while still going full speed. After practice, he said, "You know, you got to let me do better."

I said, "Dan, I'll tell you where the play is going to go. But I'm not going to look like I'm walking around out there."

He said, "Let me make my plays, and I'll let you make your plays. We're both gonna do great."

We got better at it as the season went on. As a couple of years went by, we got really good at it. One of the things that coaches always say is, "No brother-in-law." That means don't take it easy on the guy across the line to make him look good. That's what Dan and I were doing all the time. I made him look good; he made me look good.

He left the Kansas City Chiefs to sign with the Seattle Seahawks after the 1996 season. We would call each other and say, "Hey, brother-in-law!" and laugh about it. Fast forward to the Seattle rain game in 1998. We were playing in that pouring rain, and I had to play against Dan. He said, "I'm not gonna make any plays. You don't make any plays. We'll just get through this game. It's raining. Let's just get through it with nobody looking bad or looking good."

Now what do I do? This game counts. We got through the game, and maybe we cut each other some slack. Once a play was done, we just kind of stopped and talked to each other. It wasn't as blatant as practice was, but I didn't push him over any piles. And he didn't push me over any piles. We took care of each other. If there was a pile behind me, where he could push me over that pile and get me hurt, he would hold me up, and I would do the same for him.

He was my brother-in-law. Years later, I was doing a radio show. Doug Franz was my radio partner over at 610, and we got Dan on the show. I introduced Dan, "What's up, brother-in-law?"

He's like, "Yeah, brother-in-law, what's going on?"

We were laughing and joking. Doug didn't know what we're talking about, so he just went with the flow. About a month later, we had an event at the radio station, and I brought Sarah. I walked up to Franz and I said, "Doug, this my wife, Sarah. Sarah, this is Doug Franz."

A couple minutes later, he pulls me aside and says, "She's not Polynesian."

I said, "What are you talking about?"

I thought about it for a while and then I remembered my conversation with Dan.

I said, "He's not my brother-in-law. He's my *brother-in-law*."

I then had to explain the concept to Doug.

I love Dan. Even though he didn't really like practicing, I loved his zeal and his toughness in games and his nose for the football. If the ball was on the ground, Dan was going to get on it. He just had that knack. He's one of the special guys who played in the 1990s.

Tracy Simien

Tracy Simien came to the Kansas City Chiefs halfway through my rookie year. Around that time Marty Schottenheimer decided to switch sidelines for a game. We were playing against the Houston Oilers, and Marty thought because it was mid-December and that it got colder on the shade side and that we'd be on the sunny side. He thought that would keep us warmer during the game, which would give us a better opportunity to freeze out that Oilers spread offense. He thought Warren Moon and his wide receivers were going to get cold because they weren't used to it. Well, as we all know, Moon threw for 527 yards in that game, which is tied for the second most yards in a game in NFL history. The Oilers just blew us out.

I didn't know Tracy at that point. He had just joined the club and he was a linebacker, so I didn't have any reason during game prep to get to know him. I was sitting on the bench early in the game, and this guy, who wasn't even dressed, sat down next to me. He said, "So you're the center, right? Grunhard, right? I'm Tracy Simien. I've got nothing to do during this game. So I'm going to help you. I play mike [middle] linebacker and I deal with centers all the time. And I know what the defenses run. I know the defensive coordinator. I know some of the things they do.

If I give you some information and some tips during the game, I'm sure it will help."

During the game I kept hearing this voice screaming out, "Watch the mike linebacker: he's blitzing!"

He was calling everything as if he was in their huddle. He was just that kind of guy. He was just a smart football player. After the game I thanked him for the help. Obviously, we got blown out in the game. It was pathetic. But he said, "I just I want to be a part of this team. And I that was the only thing I could do."

He quickly became a big part of our defense. We had Derrick Thomas and Neil Smith as the heart of that defense in the 1990s, but Tracy was the brain of that defense. He was a smart football player and he was a great communicator. He made all the calls. He was a liaison between the defensive coordinators and the defense with Bill Maas, Dan Saleaumua, DT, and Neil. Those were all big personalities; they were all guys that had one concern—get to the ball. But somebody had to be the communicator. That's kind of what I did on my side, and that's what he did on his side. So, we had a natural bond. Tracy and I would really push each other in practice, especially when there was nobody in front of me (no nose tackle). Tracy would really do a great job of giving us a great look. When I walked onto the field in games, it was easy because I had practiced against Tracy during the week.

People don't realize that when you're playing against a team, if their mike linebacker is maybe a half a man over, or even a foot over, that's a tell. They're letting you know what they're doing. Tracy said, "Okay, I'm gonna give you those tells during practice."

Tracy was the ultimate teammate because he cared about his game. He was the leader of the defense, but then he went the extra mile, did the little things. Marty always talked about the little things. Tracy was the king of the little things.

Neil Smith and Derrick Thomas

I don't think that you could talk about the Kansas City Chiefs in the 1990s without talking about Neil Smith and Derrick Thomas. I put these two together because they combined to be the heart of the defense.

Neil had unbelievable focus on getting to the quarterback. He perfected the flinch, a technique that made offensive tackles as twitchy as a cat on a hot tin roof. It reminded me of Jackie Robinson's effect on opposing pitchers when he was at first base. Neil had a long, lanky body that could almost move in sections. He seemed to be able to move his head and shoulders on their own away from the rest of the body. This technique was so devastating, especially in Arrowhead Stadium, because the fans felt ownership of it. He was so good at it that it became illegal and a point of emphasis for the league halfway through Neil's career. If you are doing something so special that you have a rule named after you, that's pretty impressive.

Neil was never shy about this technique and talent. In fact, through social media of our time—1990s radio—he asked for assistance from his posse. He asked Chiefs fans to help him deliver. The louder the fans were, the harder it was for the tackle to be ready for Neil and the better chance he had of getting to the quarterback. Neil rewarded the fans with a patented home-run swing—in honor of local hero George Brett—after getting to the opposing quarterback.

Where do I start with second half of this dynamic duo? Derrick Thomas was the biggest playmaker on our team in the

'90s. That's right—playmaker. People refer to offensive players as playmakers. That wasn't the way we rolled in the '90s. Our playmaker was Derrick. If we needed to sack their quarterback, if we needed a safety at a crucial point in the game, his spidey senses would start to tingle, and he would pounce like a black widow.

I never met a man who loved the game of football like DT did. It was his oxygen. It was his fuel for life. DT enjoyed many things off the field, but his passion for the game was a driving force for his life. And to be brutally honest, everything was second to football—to a fault. I probably should explain that a little more. When I'm talking about the game of football, I'm talking about when the clock is running, and they're keeping score. His approach to practice was similar to Allen Iverson's feelings about practice.

That drove coaches crazy and confused many new players on the Chiefs. I can't tell you how bad DT was at practice in one-on-one pass-rush drills between offensive linemen and defensive linemen. Derrick barely went through the motions. New guys would remark that DT didn't care. I would say, "Just wait until you walk into Arrowhead Stadium on Sunday. That's his happy place."

He would not disappoint. Right before the snap, Neil and Derrick would look at each other as if to say, "See you at the quarterback." Those two would high-five many times over opposing quarterbacks. The duo started the renaissance of the Chiefs relationship with their fans in the '90s. They had outrageous radio shows together at local bars and Third and Long Foundation events that everyone attended. You probably couldn't do that today.

It didn't matter if you were the CEO of Sprint or a cashier at the local QuikTrip, you were treated with the same importance and respect. This was the spark that meant a lot to players like me. It allowed us to put our roots down in the social fabric of our hometown, Kansas City. Derrick's smile and Smith's big heart were the most influential components to my run in the social life of Kansas City. They started the rebirth and laid the first bricks in the foundation of the Chiefs Kingdom. We, as a fanbase and as a metro area, owe so much of our success to this duo. The Super Bowl was won by the Chiefs team in 2019, but the ground on which they hoisted the Lombardi Trophy was fortified by that pairing.

Derrick was my friend. I loved him like a brother. We came from different backgrounds, different cultures. We had the love for Kansas City and the love of football that made us bond. I remember, especially after losses, going to the back of the defensive bus where Neil and Derrick would be holding court with Tracy Simien, Mark Collins, and other key contributors. They'd be drinking Louis XIII cognac at $4,000 a bottle. I was allowed back by DT when I was a rookie after a certain fight with Neil Smith gave me a pass.

They would be complaining about how the offense let them down. I would listen, take a sip of my Busch Light, and take all that they could give me until it was out of their systems. Then, when the undressing was done, they would feel better. With a twinkle in his eye, DT would say, "We're all good." And that was when I knew that we could get back to work the next week.

Neil and I used to mix it up in practice quite a bit. It was kind of our thing. We were two big personalities and we would clash in the hustle of training camp. After one such incident, Neil came up to me and said, "You know, Grunny, that was kind of fun. There's nothing personal, right?"

Sometimes when we thought practices were dragging, we would look at each other and nod, and then the punches would fly WWE style. Our acting job seemed to work. Marty Schottenheimer caught on eventually; he would lower his Coke-bottle glasses and give us a knowing glance. We loved it; it was our thing.

I remember one thing from when I was a rookie. It's a tradition that rookies were told by the veteran guys to sing your college fight song at dinner. The vets, especially the defensive guys, loved to torture me almost every night. As you can imagine, this got old. At some point, after a particularly hard practice, I said "Enough" and refused.

That was just a fuel for the fire for the older guys to get on me even more. We almost came to blows right there in the cafeteria. Then, out of nowhere, I finally got an ally in DT. He jumped up and started singing his fight song. Then he said, "I think we've heard enough of that 'Cheer, Cheer for Old Notre Dame' crap." And it ended there.

My favorite moments with DT came every year at my show at The Levee. He took over the proceedings, and it was great. He and I just didn't want to go home. He was in his element with the fans. He dragged my wife, Sarah, and me along. We shared stories with the fans and had lots of laughs. Needless to say, Sarah and I found our way to the Embassy Suites up the street. We didn't have a limo on call like Derrick.

When I went to check into a room at the desk around midnight or maybe later, I asked for a room. The clerk knew who I was, but she didn't know my wife. She gave me the once over, apparently wondering who Sarah was, and then looked at Sarah, who seemed to sense this. Sarah then said, "I'm his wife." That was the first and last time that we ever did that after a radio show.

I miss my friend. I miss his smile. I miss his love for life. I miss his love for charity. That's why I always try to help DT's and Neil's charity, the Third and Long Foundation. More than 20 years after his untimely death, it's still going strong.

Those two were bookends from the defensive standpoint. But personality wise, they were about as opposite as they could be. Most people think that Derrick was the leader of those two guys. But he wasn't. Neil was the leader. He was the guy who kind of kept Derrick in line. When Neil left in free agency, Derrick struggled on and off the field. Neil knew how to keep Derrick focused and keep him in line a little bit.

Their interconnected legacy lives on. Before the epic divisional playoff game against the Buffalo Bills in January of 2022, Neil had the honor of banging the drum. He wore Derrick's No. 58 jersey while doing so.

Dave Szott

I can absolutely say that I owe my career to Dave Szott for many reasons. Some I could talk about here; some I can't. Dave was a seventh-round pick out of Penn State, another team that I love to hate. He was one of the hardest workers I ever played with in the classroom, on the field, and especially in the weight room. His workouts were legendary. Some guys would stop their own personal workouts to watch Dave finish up his feats of strength. He would do 500-pound benches and 1,000-pound squats. They were child's play for Dave. And this was a guy who put 10-pound plates in his pocket every Friday to make weight. While Derrick Graham and I would be sweating it out in a steam room to try to be under 300 pounds, which in the early '90s was the cap, he would be eating everything he could get his hands on to be over 250 pounds.

Dave learned hard work from his brother, Kevin, who set up a gym in his garage back in New Jersey. They called it Pig Street, which was named after the famous Harlem boxing gym.

Kevin was legally blind, but he never let that get in the way of excelling in every sport he ever tried, especially judo. When he competed in the Paralympic Games, Dave was inspired. He was pushed by the fact that you couldn't make excuses or complain about hard work. That didn't fly with Kevin.

Since he was a late-round pick, Dave barely got any reps in training camp. The first preseason game that Dave and I started next to each other our rookie year was against the New York Jets. They had a great defensive line with guys like Jeff Lageman, Scott Mersereau, Ron Stallworth, and Marvin Washington. They took it to us. We both thought we were going to get cut. I didn't think they were going to cut me because I was a second-round draft choice. But I thought my boy may be in trouble. So we hid. We went to Mountain Home, Arkansas, and went fishing on the White River. We thought if they were unable to find us, they couldn't cut us. The next Monday, we went in separately. I was nervous for my friend. But Dave didn't get cut. He not only made the team, but he also had an unbelievable career.

Dave and I lived together for our first two years in the league. We could write a book on the adventures of two city kids from Chicago and Clifton, New Jersey, respectively, on a ranch in Missouri. We'd have you in stitches. That's what we shared on the radio shows together. We let people into our personal lives. It was like the fans were sitting around the campfire and listening to two old cowpokes opining on our daily adventures. Yes, we talked football and we broke down the next opponent. But we let fans in. We would poke fun of each other in a self-deprecating way. Joe Fan knew that we were the same as he or she was. We made the same dumb mistakes. Just because we wore the red and gold of the Chiefs on Sunday didn't mean that we didn't do obnoxious things the other six days of the week. Dave was my soulmate. He was the closest person to me other than my wife, Sarah, throughout my career.

I can't narrow my favorite moments with Dave down to one. Every time I was tired during the game, I knew I could look over to my friend next to me. He was a guy I trusted. I knew he had my back and I knew he cared. It got me through the tough times in the game. I was blessed to have characters like Dave in my life.

Chiefs Kingdom was not built with a bunch of robots but by a bunch of characters. Two stories demonstrate that. One time Dave and I were fishing in Canada with John Alt. We were doing a fly-in adventure. We took a sea plane, and they came out in these old boats to pick you up. You had to jump from the plane into the boat. John had a bad back, which made it difficult for him to get in and out of the boat. John's father was in a really bad car accident when John was a baby and was paralyzed from the waist down. Through different infections, he lost both legs.

John was helping his father get into the boat and he got a cramp in his back, causing him to throw his dad up in the air. His dad would have sunk like a like a rock to the bottom of this lake in the middle of Canada, but Dave caught John's dad as he was flying over the edge of the boat. Dave grabbed him and put him in the boat. "Yeah, my back was crap," John said.

I said, "But you almost threw your dad into the water."

Dave also borrowed Bill Maas' tractor. We had moved out to Lee's Summit, Missouri, where I had about 20 acres of grass. I bought this house during my rookie year. I let Dave live with me. And I told him he didn't have pay me any money, but he had to do some chores around the house. Of course, being a city kid, I forgot that grass actually does grow. In the spring I had nothing to cut the 20 acres of grass that was basically in front of my house. It quickly started to look like some wild pasture, and I'm sure the neighbors were none too happy about it. So I hired this guy to come and cut the grass, which was costing me a ton of money. So Billy Bob said, "Just come over and borrow my tractor until you get your own. You don't have to pay all that money."

So I drove Dave over to Bill's house, which was about four or five miles away. After an hour or two—then three—went by, there was still no sight of Dave. I had no idea what happened. Did Dave stay at Bill's house? Did he get in an accident? So I drove toward Bill's house. There's a big hill, and Dave was going like 2 miles per hour down the road. There was a line of traffic that had to be a half mile long. I pulled him over said, "What are you doing?"

He said, "This is as fast as it goes."

He was driving it in low gear. He was pushing the gas as much as he could, but it wasn't going anywhere. Bill must have thought there was no way this guy was that dumb that he wouldn't put it in high to drive it. The tractor was burning up. We got it back to the house and decided we'd better let it sit and cool down a little bit.

I got up in the morning and the grass wasn't cut. Instead of waiting on Dave, I decided I was going to do it, which was a mistake. All of a sudden, I lost control of the tractor and went flying into the pond. Bill was not too happy that we not only burned his tractor up, but we also submerged it into a pond. We end up buying him a new tractor.

The ranch that Dave and I shared was the source of many interesting stories. Remember we're two city boys who decided we wanted to live in the country. Bad idea. I thought it would be cool to get a horse. There was a guy that owned a horse ranch with a bunch of horses behind us. It was connected to the back of our land. So I put a little gate in there, where I could bring the horse back and forth. When I wasn't home, I could bring it over there, and he would take care of it. The horse's name was Copper. We decided we were going to Westport one night like many 23-year-old kids would do. We got back at about 2:00 AM. We decided to check on the horse and we saw the horse laying down in the pasture. We thought, *That can't be good.*

We noticed that he broke into the stall with the grain and ate 40 pounds of grain. A horse will eat itself to death if you let it. It doesn't have any governor when it comes to eating. I was freaking out, thinking this horse was going to die. There was an old veterinarian who lived across the street. He had said, "Any time you have any issues, give me a call."

It was 3:30 AM, and I called the vet across the street. He was none too pleased, but I thought the horse was going to die. I identified myself and told him what had happened. He said the only option we had was to take a hose and "stick it where the sun don't shine and get some warm water in there." The goal was to hopefully flush it out. I looked at Dave, and he looked at me. I said, "I'm not sticking the hose up that horse's rear."

He said, "I'm not doing it either."

We decided we'd get in my dad's old pickup truck and chase Copper. We thought if we scared it, it might jump up and start running around. We pulled up to the horse in the pasture and started beeping the horn and flashing the lights. The horse was groaning and rolling. I got up really close and roared the engine, and Cooper jumped up. The next thing I know, it explosively crapped all over the windshield of the truck. Once we got it going, we decided to chase it around the pasture. We were honking the horn, trying to bump it, keeping it moving. We figured the more it ran, the more it would shoot out grain everywhere. I'm surprised that we didn't wreck the truck.

The next morning, the veterinarian came by. When he walked into the pasture, there was the pickup truck full of horse crap. It looked like it was just in a tornado of crap. He said, "I've been a vet for 50 years and I've never seen anything like that."

Buying a ranch had been my dream ever since I was a kid. When I grew up in Chicago, I could reach out my window in my bedroom and touch the house next door. I thought if I ever made any money, I wanted to live on a ranch. It was one of those childhood dreams that probably should have remained a dream. When I married Sarah, she came in and straightened everything out. But it was so much work. Let me say I'll never do that again.

Mike Webster

I have two regrets when it comes to my football career. One was never being able to hand Lamar Hunt the trophy that was named after him. Yes, a Super Bowl is the ultimate goal, but the thought of not being able to hand the Lamar Hunt Trophy to Lamar haunts me to this day. The other regret is not knowing the extent of Mike Webster's struggles or being able to help my mentor. Mike was the kindest man I ever met. He took me under his wing and gave me the confidence to play in this league for 11 years.

The first time I met Mike, he was a shell of his gladiator self who brought multiple Super Bowls to the Pittsburgh Steelers.

His body couldn't do it anymore. His football mind still had one more step to give, and he gave that to me. Mike was sitting in a cold tub, the place where he made his home in the locker room, when I first met him. He said, "So you're the guy that I'm going to pass the keys to the huddle to?"

I didn't get it. But as I learned through the years, it is the quarterback who is the driver of the car. But it's the center who—along with his four partners—is the engine. He said, "Do what I tell you, kid, and maybe we can figure out what kind of player you're going to be."

So this big-mouthed, brash, young hotshot from Notre Dame had to learn to keep his mouth shut and listen. The first thing he told me was that my job was to set the tempo of the huddle. Never shirk your responsibilities. Run to the line of scrimmage, and the offensive line will eventually follow you. Finish every play to the whistle. When the circumstances warrant, help up the guy with the ball and sprint back to the huddle. I thought that was crazy. I'd be tuckered out by the second quarter. But he was right.

The other thing he stressed was to always know the difference between pain and injury. We played through pain. Pain is a mind-set. And it's always there if you want to use it as an excuse. But if you do, you no longer trust yourself when times get tough. We all know this is not sustainable mentally, and Mike paid for it. The speed at which he did things was unbelievable. Not only did he still push out a ton of iron, but he did it running full speed from one apparatus to the next. It was intimidating to watch this 38-year-old man blow through the weight room. It was like the Tasmanian devil. Everything he did, he did full speed.

Halfway through the 1990 season, my father passed away. I was kind of going through that struggle, and Mike was there for me. He organized a collection for my mom. He called me just about every day to see how I was doing. When I got back from the funeral, I tore my thumb. I had this big cast on my hand. So, I was going through some tough times. Besides that, I hit the rookie wall.

The rookie wall was a real thing mentally and physically. You feel it's time to shut it down because in college you played 12 games at the most. Well, if you count preseason and regular season games, that's halfway through an NFL season. You've got to bust through it. Some guys can, and some guys can't. So I was not only suffering through the hand injury and rookie wall, but I also had my father pass away. I tried to play with the cast on my hand.

We were playing a game against the Denver Broncos, and in the first half, I just couldn't do anything right. I got called for holding. I got beat for a sack. And the mistakes were starting to feed off each other. In the middle of like the fourth or fifth series, I got this tap on my shoulder. It was Mike. He said Marty Schottenheimer wanted me to take a break and he was going to replace me. Let me preface it by saying you don't pull offensive linemen in the middle of a series. I'd never seen it happen before and I've pretty much never seen it happen after. I was sitting on the bench, thinking, *I just lost my dad, I've got this big cast on my hand, I just bought this house, I'm gonna get cut.* All this crap was going through my mind, and I was pouting.

At halftime I sat at my locker, very dejected. I looked over, and Mike was taking his shoes off. I figured he was probably going to get retaped. Next thing you know, he took off his jersey. Marty noticed this and said, "Webby, what are you doing?"

Mike said, "I'm not going back in. That's your guy. He's got to get back on the horse, he needs to go play. You need to trust in him. I trust him."

He looked at me and said, "You need to go play and get out of this funk."

At that point, I was like, *Mike Webster believes in me so much that he would take his equipment off and say, "I'm giving you the keys."*

It was like *Rocky II* when Adrian wakes up and says, "Win, Rocky!" Mickey stands up and says, "What are we waiting for?"

The light bulb went off in my brain. I knew I could do it. I went out on the field and had a great second half. It was a complete 180. Somebody important believed in me, and it just kind of kicked me into gear. I broke that rookie wall down. I believe I owe my career to Mike. Because if it was any other guy, he probably would have continued to play, and I would have continued to pout. If I would have gone back in the game, I probably would have started playing badly again.

That one act of kindness saved my career. People always ask me why I coach high school football. I could be doing anything. I could be doing color commentating or working in the business world. I just always point back to the time Mike invested in me and saved my career. He gave me an opportunity to play this sport. And now I want to be there for some kid. I don't know who it's going to be. I don't know if they'll recognize it. But if I say something or do something that pays Mike back for what he did for me, then I've accomplished something.

I just feel so bad that I didn't know what he was going through. Nobody really knew. I was the closest person to him. I went over to his house for Thanksgiving with his family, and Sarah and I went over there for Christmas. I knew that he had some quirks and some issues, but I had no idea of the extent of his issues. If I would have known how bad it was, I would have been out there looking for him in Pittsburgh. I would have done anything. Many people have seen the movie *Concussion*, which focused on much of Mike's story. I don't know how much of it is true, but if any of it is even close, it's just a heartbreaker that he had to go through that.

My Favorite Games

I PLAYED IN 169 GAMES IN MY 11-YEAR CAREER, INCLUDING START-
ing in 164 of them. It seems ludicrous to pick a handful of games
as my favorites. I loved playing the game, and it's hard to put
one game in front of another as a favorite. I mean, I have four
kids and I can't figure out who are the top three, so how could
I rank my 169 games? But unlike my former teammates in the
last chapter, I'm not only going to attempt to pick my favorite
games. I'm going to rank them from my fifth favorite down to the
first. But I'm going to cheat a little and do a few combinations.

No. 5
Los Angeles Raiders, 1991
The Kansas City Chiefs played the Los Angeles Raiders in back-
to-back weeks in 1991.

The final game of the regular season was played in the Los
Angeles Coliseum. Both teams had already clinched a playoff
berth, but neither team had a chance to win the AFC West. The
winner of the game in Los Angeles would host the wild-card
game the next weekend.

The Chiefs won the first game, which meant we'd host a
postseason game for the first time since the Christmas Day game
in 1971—20 seasons earlier. The Chiefs then beat the Raiders

at Arrowhead in the playoffs, the first postseason victory since Super Bowl IV and the *first home playoff win* in franchise history. All three of their AFL Championships were won on the road—in 1962 (the Dallas Texans against the Houston Oilers in Houston), in 1966 (the Chiefs against the Buffalo Bills in Buffalo), and 1969 (the Chiefs against the New York Jets in New York and then the Oakland Raiders in Oakland).

But in order for that opportunity to happen, the Chiefs had to beat the Raiders on the road. That was a must-win for both teams. Going into the game, we knew if we won the game, we'd play a home game at Arrowhead Stadium. That was important to us because obviously in the previous 20 years or so there weren't any playoff games in Kansas City. For us to turn the page and start moving to where we wanted to go, we knew we had to win that game. It was a back-and-forth game, even though we never trailed. There were no turnovers on either side. The Raiders fans were just as crazy as ever, but we just kept on playing.

Our quarterback, Steve DeBerg, completed 14-of-20 passes for 277 yards and two touchdowns. Barry Word rushed for 152 yards, and receiver J.J. Birden caught eight passes for 188 yards and two touchdowns. It was an offensive lineman's dream; the Chiefs didn't have to punt and we held the ball for almost 40 minutes. One of the things I do remember about that game was Marty Schottenheimer's preparation. Coach would always talk about how the Raiders would self-destruct. The Raiders always seemed to commit penalties or make other mistakes at key moments. That was kind of their trademark.

I will never forget Dave Szott, one of the quietest and most reserved guys on the team, was asked the question from one of the media members in Kansas City about what he thought about the game. He kind of alluded to the fact that the Raiders would self-destruct. That was bulletin-board material for the Raiders. Marty didn't really know about Dave's comments until we walked into the locker room before the game. Somebody made a comment to Dave about it, and Marty heard it and he said, "What was that all about?"

Dave said, "I guess I made the mistake of talking about some of the things we talked about in the meeting."

That's the last thing you need in a rivalry game: to give the other team bulletin-board material.

The Raiders really didn't self-destruct in that game. They had no turnovers and only six penalties. They scored two touchdowns in the fourth quarter and needed only one more touchdown to win. Maybe that was the point of emphasis for them in that game—to make sure they didn't have a lot of penalties or turn the ball over.

They must have forgotten about avoiding miscues as they went into the playoff game the next week. You have to remember that this became another "Raiders Week." Marty always made it a point of emphasis when we played the Raiders. When you walked out of the tunnel, there were signs that said, "Raiders Week." When you walked into the weight room, there were signs that said, "Raiders Week." When you walked into the training room, there was all kinds of stuff reminding us that we were playing against the Raiders. One of Marty's things was that we had to beat our rival. We had to beat the Raiders. He didn't have a lot of respect for Al Davis because he felt that Davis didn't respect the Chiefs organization. He didn't care if Davis liked the Chiefs. He wanted Davis to respect the brand, to respect the badge, to respect the shield of the NFL.

In the second game, you could tell there was a difference. I always tell people that in the NFL there is a difference between the intensity of the regular season and the postseason. It's like a 10-speed bike: you click it to a speed and you pedal. But when you click it up to the next speed, things pick up. In training camp you have one speed. If you're a young guy, you think it's fast. As you go into the preseason, it steps up. Once you go into the regular season, it picks up another step. The speed of the game and the knowledge that you need picks up another step because it's that much quicker. When you get in the playoffs, the speed picks up even more. So does the intensity. When we walked into the locker room after that win in L.A., there was a different feeling. There was a different intensity in that locker room than I had ever experienced. Yes, we had played in a playoff game the year before, but we were going to host a home playoff game against the Raiders.

All week long, Marty talked about the history of the Raiders and the Chiefs. Marty wanted us to understand why this game was important to Kansas City and to Chiefs fans. Mostly, he wanted us to know why this game was important to Lamar Hunt. Every meeting started out with a history lesson about different games and different people who played in the game and differ-ent situations that had happened over the years that made this a great rivalry. So there was a lot of intensity.

During the playoff week, Marty really emphasized Davis. He said, "Al Davis is going to walk onto the field and he is not going to have any respect for any of you. He is not going to have any respect for Lamar Hunt who is up in his suite. He is not going to have any respect for the Kansas City Chiefs' fans. He does not like the Chiefs and he doesn't respect us."

Marty didn't recognize the rivalry when he first arrived in Kansas City, a year before I did. My coauthor told me about the week leading up to the first Chiefs–Raiders game in 1989, which was the home opener. On a telephone interview with other media members, David asked Marty a question like, "You're an old AFL guy. Is there any significance to the Chiefs/Raiders rivalry?"

Marty said, "No, none at all. That's an old AFL rivalry. The Chiefs haven't been good." He basically downplayed the whole thing.

That game was a back-and-forth game where the lead changed hands five times. The Chiefs scored in the fourth quarter to win 24–19. In the postgame press conference, Marty sat there with his Diet Coke and his hands were shaking.

They opened it up for questions, and David raised his hand and said, "Marty, is this game special?"

He just said, "Oh, yeah." That's when he recognized that this rivalry was just as good as it used to be.

Before the playoff game against the Raiders, Coach Schottenheimer played the respect card all week long, and it worked. We were really ready for that game. We were very excited for that game. We came out clicking. It was a gray day. It was weird; the gray of the Raiders helmets just accentuated the atmosphere. It was a gray, dreary day in Kansas City. So when we started out, it was all about setting the tempo. What was Marty's point of emphasis all week? It was controlling the football, running the ball right down their throats, and taking it to them.

That's what we did on that very first drive. We drove down on a 15- or 16-play drive of mostly runs. We had three or four third-down conversions and a fourth-down conversion. They made a good stop to force a field goal; they had a really good defense after all. In kind of a microcosm of my career in Kansas

City, Nick Lowery missed the field goal, so we came off the field kind of dejected.

There were really two stars in the game, and they were both on the defensive side. One of them was obviously Derrick Thomas. He always played well in playoff games and he always played well against the Raiders. He had another one of his great games. But Deron Cherry was the difference-maker. Deron discovered by watching film that Raiders quarterback Todd Marinovich had a tendency of looking at his intended receiver first. He tried to look away, but he always went back. Deron picked that up and had a couple of interceptions in that game, and it was all connected to him doing his homework and understanding the little tendencies of the quarterback.

That game was once again a perfect microcosm of that 1991 season. The only touchdown was a one-handed, play-action pass that DeBerg made famous because he was so good at it. He learned it from Roger Staubach when he was in training camp with the Dallas Cowboys. He ran that play-action and threw the ball to Fred Jones for the one touchdown.

The defense played unbelievably well. Marinovich threw four interceptions and lost two fumbles. They also had nine penalties. The Raiders' tendency to self-destruct was very real. It was just delayed a week. Kevin Ross, who was the ultimate gamesman and a psychological player, went up to Marinovich after one of the interceptions and whispered in his ear. I never knew what he said, but you could tell Marinovich was just devastated.

That game was The Barry Word Show. Marty liked a running-back-by-committee approach, but in that game, it was all Word. He had 130 of the Chiefs' 131 yards rushing. The Raiders actually outgained us, but we did all the little things right. It was Martyball to a T: play solid defense, get turnovers, avoid penalties, control the line of scrimmage, run the ball, and take shots using play-action passes. That's what propelled us to a playoff victory against the Raiders.

As a young football player, you always think there are going to be plenty more of these opportunities. Winning a game at home at Arrowhead Stadium in front of those fans had a different feel from the fans that week. They understood this was a home playoff game, the first in 20 years. I walked off the football field believing that Arrowhead had played a role. Arrowhead turned into that legendary place that they talk about now with decibels and the loudest stadium. Well, the birth of that place for me was that playoff game against the Raiders. The fans were into it. They were excited. They knew it was an important game for us. They knew it was a home playoff game, the first home play-off game in a long, long time and against the Raiders. It was a perfect storm. The fans certainly weathered that storm and they caused a lot of the thunder and lightning that happened during that game. The Raiders couldn't hear anything. Marinovich was flustered, and it started pre-snap with the fans' noise.

We knew that we had made strides in Kansas City, that the fans were starting to buy in, that the fans understood that there was something different in this generation of the Chiefs. We had a sense of Missouri—the "Show-Me State." We had to show them. The playoff game was a great opportunity to walk on a stage and show them. Even though it was the playoffs and on national television, it wasn't a national stage. It wasn't even a regional stage for us. It was a Kansas City stage.

I felt like that game was the first game where we kind of reached across the aisle. The feeling was: let's bring this together, let's shake hands, we're in this together, this is our team. This is Kansas City's team. If you talk with people about some of their fondest memories of Chiefs games in the '90s, they'll bring up that playoff game because it was like turning the page. The '80s were a rough time for the Chiefs and Chiefs fans, though they were gritty. They needed the team to turn the page and reach across the aisle and say, "Come with us, let's go." That's what happened in that game.

The other thing that really stuck in my mind was it was the first time that I had the opportunity to watch Marcus Allen run the football. There were only a couple of guys that I had stood up and watched as a player. Usually, you're on the bench, drinking water, or maybe talking to the guys when your defense is on the field, but Barry Sanders and Marcus were two guys that I would stand up and watch. Marcus had a nice game against us in the first game.

The other thing about that game was the matchup with our quarterback, DeBerg, and the Raiders' rookie quarterback, Marinovich. DeBerg was one of the oldest guys in the NFL at that point, and Marinovich was the youngest quarterback. The NFL is all about quarterback play. We felt like we had an advantage, even though Marinovich played pretty well against us in the game in Los Angeles. But he had to come to Kansas City on a cold, gray day and had to play against an old, gray quarterback in DeBerg.

No. 4
San Francisco 49ers, 1994 and 1997

When we talk about big games against the San Francisco 49ers, the first game that jumps to mind is the Joe Montana versus Steve Young game in 1994. Of course, there was Super Bowl LIV, but I didn't play in that one. (I would have suited up if they asked me, but it's probably good that they didn't.)

In 1997 we both had really good records. We were 9–3, and the 49ers were 11–1. We had lost Elvis Grbac, who used to play for the 49ers, a couple weeks before, so this was Rich Gannon's opportunity to walk on the field and shine for the Kansas City Chiefs. One reason I remember this game is because later on in the season it caused the controversy when Grbac got healthy. Marty Schottenheimer had a policy that you didn't lose your starting position because of injury. As a player, I appreciated that. But there were times that it backfired. I think this is one of those times.

But back to the game in 1997. The 49ers were an excellent football team with Steve Young at quarterback. They were favored at Arrowhead partly because we were going to play our backup. But Rich went out there and played awesome. We scored 44 points against them and held them to three field goals. It was a thorough spanking of the 49ers. "We got punched in the mouth," Young said to the media afterward.

The game speaks for itself. It was never close. Our defense dominated up front. They were all over Young the whole game. The Chiefs offensive line were our offensive players of the week. That was fun because John Madden was doing the color commentary for the game, and that propelled me to become an All-Madden football player.

We just ran up and down field on them. The 49ers had won 11 consecutive games, the last 10 by at least a touchdown. After having just destroyed people that whole season, they only managed 127 yards rushing and 152 yards passing.

There is another reason I remember this game. I wasn't one of those guys who went to prayer meetings before games. I was religious and went to mass, but I didn't go to the Fellowship of Christian Athletes services before games. That week I remember walking into the locker room and I just kind of felt something like, *You should go to this service.* I walked in. Everybody kind of looked around, kind of surprised that I was there. It was weird. I just felt a pull, a calling. I was one of those guys who just prayed to win. I know you're not supposed to pray for wins. You're supposed to pray that everybody stays healthy. But I remember going in there and thinking, *Okay, God, I'll make a deal with you. I'll go to these meetings the rest of my career if you help us win this football game.*

This was 1997. I was in my eighth season and I had never gone to one. From the beginning of the game, I had a spiritual experience. It was a bright and sunny day. The fans were all dressed in red. It just looked like a sea of red. They were loud and boisterous. They didn't like the 49ers either. Rich was so inspirational in the huddle. He was so calm, cool, and collected. Anything he said or did—or anything he tried to do—was accomplished. It was a spiritual experience for me. For some reason in that game, everything I tried, I did right.

I've talked before about how the souls of the players and the fans connected in Kansas City, and that is what happened here. If I went back on all the games that I have played, that game more than any other for some reason may have connected me with the fans, my teammates, and with the game. It was transformational for me, a unique experience. It made me realize how blessed I was to play this game. It made me feel how blessed I was to play in front of those fans. It made me feel how blessed I was to have the teammates that I had and the experience that I had in Kansas City.

I am a man of my word and for the rest of my career I went to the chapel service every week. Some were more inspirational than others, but I did go. I made that deal and I figured I wasn't going against that. I really enjoyed it. It kind of gave me a focus and was something that I enjoyed going to. The last three-and-a half years, I went to all of them. It was a different way of preparing for me. The older I got, I needed that. I realized that with that second 49ers game.

The other thing that I remember about that game in 1997 was a feeling among the guys who were part of the team in 1994. I think a lot of people thought that the only reason we beat the 49ers in 1994 was because we had Joe Montana. The 49ers were probably the best football team in the '90s. The thought by many so-called experts was that we beat them because we took one of their guys.

But in 1997 we went on the field without Montana. We didn't even have our starting quarterback, Elvis Grbac, but we were going out to battle the 49ers with Rich. During the week leading up to the game, we talked about the fact that their defensive line was really good. They were putting a lot of pressure on opposing quarterbacks. They were also doing really well against the run. But look at the stats. Rich was not sacked at all in that game, while Young was sacked five times. We had the ball 10 more minutes and we ran 19 more plays than the 49ers. It was just one of those games where there was a special unity and a spiritual connection in that game.

The game against the 49ers in 1994 was one of the most hyped games I've ever been in. It was like the Miami versus Notre Dame game I played in during my junior year in college. It was just the second game of the NFL season, and both teams came in 1–0. The hype was all about Young versus Montana, even though those two guys were never on the field at the same time. The hype was national. It focused on the two quarterbacks. Joe had been with us for a season and he didn't want the focus to be on him. He wanted it to be just another game. At least, that's what he said. There were times where he made a big play or came off after a touchdown and there was a special twinkle in his eye. You could tell that he was excited about beating Young.

Unlike when Grbac got hurt three years later for the Chiefs, when Montana got hurt, Young took his job. It wasn't Young's fault, but Joe felt like he earned the right to take that job back, and they didn't give it to him. That's one of the reasons he left San Francisco. There may have been a little animosity between the two, but Joe tried to tamp that down as much as possible. ESPN had a story just about every day going into that game about Joe. We had national media all over our locker room. All the talking heads from ESPN and CBS were all there covering the game from the beginning of the week.

While the national narrative was about a matchup game between Montana and Young, it really turned out to be a matchup between their offensive line and Derrick Thomas. DT carried the day. He was our playmaker. He played like his pants were on fire. He had three sacks. Then, after a couple of offensive penalties put the 49ers on their own 7-yard line, Derrick sacked Young for a safety. It kind of changed the feel of that game. We were down 14–7 at the time, and that made it 14–9. Our defense was on. They told us at halftime, "Steve Young is not getting any more points."

It was one of those games where we were struggling a little bit on offense. Derrick kind of kicked us into gear. After the safety we came out and said, "We've got this, we've just got to keep doing what we're doing."

We scored on our opening possession of the second half and got the two-point conversion. Charles Mincy then intercepted Young, which set up a Marcus Allen touchdown, and we had a 24–14 lead. The 49ers could only muster a field goal in the second half, and we ended up winning 24–17.

There were probably some people that thought Young would lead the 49ers back. He could be the next Montana, the comeback kid. He couldn't do it. Our team refused to let him do that. Montana was the comeback kid, not Young. Our defense went out there and made it a point of emphasis; they were not going to let Young go down and score on a last-second drive. That was a Montana trait, not a Young trait.

Joe obviously had some animosity toward the 49ers for not giving him the opportunity to regain his starting spot. But I'm not sure that it carried over to Young. There was a healthy competition between the two, and I don't think they were going out to lunch together or playing 18 holes of golf together. There were times when Joe would say that Young would go in and push the blame on other people. Joe just didn't do that. That was one of the things that Joe was never fond of with Young: that he didn't take a lot of personal responsibility for the things that he did wrong. Joe always did.

I'll tell you that very few quarterbacks will tell the coach that a quarterback/center exchange was the quarterback's fault. They always blame the center. That's the way it is. Joe always blamed himself. Even if it was a bad snap because it slipped out of my hand because of moisture or sweat or even it was just during a practice, Joe always took responsibility. That was one thing that bothered him about Young, and we all knew that.

I will never forget at the end of that game in the locker room, Marty Schottenheimer gave the game ball to Joe. All the other guys were excited for him, and he took it with a big smile on his face. Maybe it wasn't the Lombardi Trophy, but it was darn close. He was that excited about getting that ball and winning that football game. Joe Cool did not want to show his cards all week, but he laid his cards down on the table after that game. He was excited and happy to go out and beat his old team, a team that gave up on him, a team that decided the other guy was better, a team that did what nobody ever does—give your position to someone else because of injury—and they did all those things to maybe the best quarterback in the history of the NFL.

That was as happy as I've seen him in all the years that he played—even in playoff games. He was really happy. Joe Cool let down his guard a little bit, and we saw a little kid in Joe Montana. He may not have embraced the hype before the game, but it was really important to the rest of us to get Joe that win. He had decided to come to Kansas City. He had decided to be a part of our team. Maybe it was because he didn't have a lot of options, including staying with the 49ers. But he chose Kansas City. We wanted to pay him back.

He brought a lot of excitement. He brought a lot of great moments to us. He was a great leader in the locker room. He was a fun guy to be around. He was a superstar player, and I think the players felt like he'd given us so much that maybe we could turn around and give him something back.

No. 3
Buffalo Bills, 1991

This was the coming-out party for the Kansas City Chiefs.

It was the night where we were introduced to the nation and to the average NFL fan. It was the first time the Kansas City Chiefs were at home on *Monday Night Football* in a very, very long time. We played against a Buffalo Bills team that was *the* AFC team of the '90s. They were the defending AFC champions and were undefeated at 5–0. They had the best offense in the league, and the defense was really stingy, too.

All week it felt different. The older guys were telling the younger guys, "Even your kindergarten teacher is going to watch you play tonight. Everybody that you've ever known is going to watch this game."

It was a national TV game. All the players on all the other teams were putting their feet up and watching to see what we were all about. That adds a little bit of pressure, but it was a great experience. Driving into that game, it just felt different. It was almost a Phil Collins, "In the Air Tonight" kind of feeling. You could "feel it coming in the air tonight." (Now that song is stuck in your head. Sorry.)

Chiefs fans were at a different level. The tailgating was at a different level. The brightness of the red was at a different level. Just driving in and seeing the smoke billow over the stadium from the tailgates and seeing the excitement of thousands of people all over the parking lot who were getting themselves mentally ready for this game was fun. The hair stood up on your arms driving into the game. It was like a game where you run out onto the field, and you have that adrenaline and that sensation of *Wow, this is really cool.* That was how we all felt just *driving* into the stadium. So, we all knew it was going to be a special night.

Before the game it was as quiet in the locker room as I can remember. Guys understood the importance of this game. They understood the importance of getting the Chiefs on the NFL map. It just felt different from the minute you drove into the complex to the minute that you got to your locker to the minute that you ran out on that field, and it was loud. They have the decibel level on scoreboards or videoboards now to get everybody pumped up. They didn't need to do that in that game. It was as loud as I've ever heard in a stadium. I've played in some big stadiums in some big games, and that was the loudest. That's where Arrowhead Stadium got its reputation as being the loudest stadium from that game on national TV.

It was the culmination of the Marty Schottenheimer/Carl Peterson experiment that connected the fans with the players. This was more than gameday for the players. This was the test. *Can we connect with the fans? Can the fans connect with us? Can they be a difference maker? Can they influence the game?* Without a doubt all of that happened in this game. There was a lot of pride in the fanbase because they felt like they were participants in that game. They weren't just spectators. With the backing of Lamar Hunt, the mad scientist of Carl wanted the fans to feel like they had a role that they really didn't have before.

The place went crazy. Everything went the Chiefs' way because of the crowd. It was the first time that the crowd walked out of the stadium, thinking, *We were a part of this win.* In my mind, the focus was how to recreate that. There were times when we did and times when we didn't. That was always the goal. The bar was set that night against Buffalo.

Buffalo was the first team to go with the hurry-up offense. The Bills were having a lot of success against other teams. When a team uses the hurry-up on offense, the defense can't make substitutions or really change their schemes or personnel. That was their advantage. They were undefeated and were the No. 1 offense in the league at that point.

That was very unusual back then. Teams always huddled, the quarterback called the play, and the offense went to the line of scrimmage and snapped the ball with about eight to 10 seconds left. Buffalo's offense was set up for Jim Kelly to call the play at the line of scrimmage, trying to snap the ball with about 15 to

20 seconds left. That's how fast they wanted to go. Kelly used to talk about that all the time: "the faster we go, the more the defense is on their heels."

Because of the crowd, the Bills couldn't do that that night. That was the first sign that this was going to be a little bit different for them. They could not call their offense the way they wanted to, and it affected them. The Arrowhead Stadium crowd made the difference. Those fans took away that advantage, and our defense destroyed them. They had five turnovers and allowed six sacks. Marty said he could tell from warmups that the crowd was going to be a factor because the crowd was so alive that it made the hair stand up on his arms.

Martyball was in a perfect situation to have success. He wanted to dictate the action to the opponent, which is hard to do when the opponent is running a hurry-up offense. The other thing that he wanted to do was run the ball. In that game Christian Okoye had 122 yards, and Harvey Williams had 103 yards. We rushed for almost 240 yards in that game. It was quintessential Martyball. Heading into the third quarter it was 13–6, so it was still kind of close. But we started to wear them down, and that's what Martyball is all about.

With Marytball it may be a little close in the first quarter. The other team may even have the advantage in the first quarter. But by the second quarter, everything is equal. And we always said that by the third quarter, the opponents were going to feel it, and by the fourth quarter, they're going to quit because Martyball was all about pounding, pounding, pounding, wearing them out. In the fourth quarter, we went about our business, and they couldn't hold up.

We always talk about Martyball being an offensive thing, but that was really a defensive thing, too. The Bills took out Kelly midway through the fourth quarter. The game wasn't technically over; Buffalo could have come back, but they had quit because our defense was so dominant. One of the things that Marty always wanted to do was ramp things up on defense in the red zone. Whenever Buffalo got into the red zone, not only did the crowd get crazy, but all of a sudden, the defense pinned its ears back and shut down the Bills. They scored only two field goals. That wasn't what they were used to doing. I was shocked with how much we dominated them. This was the best team in the league, the reigning AFC champs. And we won 33–6.

Very few people remember the play of the offensive line in that game or any game. But that game was kind of a payback for me. There was a game within a game for me. During my freshman year at Notre Dame, I was thrown into the fire in Birmingham, Alabama. It was about 120 degrees on that turf as we played the University of Alabama. There is a famous play in Alabama football history, the famous sack by Cornelius Bennett. He bull rushed the tackle and destroyed Steve Beuerlein. There are pictures of that sack all over the football complex at Alabama. I had to go into the game after that play. The crowd was going crazy, and it was hot. Here came this freshman, who had never really played, going against probably the best defensive end in America. He never let up on me at all. I don't think I even touched him on a couple of plays. After that game I said, "Either I've got to get better or give up."

It was a growing moment for me. I knew I needed to get out of my comfort zone and work on a lot of things if I wanted to get where I needed to go. I knew what I needed to do in order to compete against that kind of player, not only to play at a high level in college, but also if I wanted to play in the NFL. So I made the adjustments I needed to make in the weight room and training to get better. All that hard work and dedication and all those adjustments, all those things, kind of came to a head in this game. I was in my second year in the NFL, and because of an injury to the starter, Bennett had to play the mike linebacker right over the center. That wasn't his position. I was licking my chops because I knew he was out of position, and this was my payback. It worked out well.

We ran for all those yards, and he didn't feel comfortable without having the space he usually had. When I got at him, I was relentless. After the game, he found me and said, "What was that all about?"

He wasn't happy because I was pushing him a little bit past the whistle—not much past but maybe a little bit past it.

I said, "Payback is a bitch," and he had no idea what I was talking about. I reminded him of the game at Alabama when I was a freshman. He kind of snickered and walked off.

The Chiefs had a coming-out party in that 1991 Buffalo game, and I kind of had my own coming-out party because I exorcised those demons of playing against Bennett when I was a freshman.

I also want to thank Rick Sutcliffe for an assist in that game. The former All-Star pitcher, who was born outside Kansas City, may or may not have taken some of the Bills' star players out to dinner the night before. He may or may not have caused them to miss curfew by quite a bit. Maybe that had a little bit of effect on their play the next day. It just felt like the plan came together perfectly that night. The gameplan for the organization in the '90s was not only to win football games, but also to win over the fanbase and to make the fans feel like they were a part of this team, and that was kind of when the fans and the players kind of reached across the aisle and grabbed hands and said, "Let's do this together."

No. 2

Houston Oilers, 1993

In 1993 we lost 30–0 to the Houston Oilers in Week Two. Joe Montana was out. Two or three offensive linemen were out. There were some defensive guys out. So, with only a few healthy starters on the offensive line, we knew we were in for a long day, especially against Buddy Ryan, who was famous for creating the 46 defense. Their 46 defense was all about covering up the guys in the middle and attacking from the edges. It used really athletic linebackers to do so. It was a stifling defense. There was all kinds of movement, slants, stunts, blitzes. You name it; they did it.

That's what made the Chicago Bears famous in 1985. That was the defense that Ryan was running in Houston in 1993 with a pretty good crew, maybe as good as the Bears' defense in '85. The Oilers team won 11 straight games to finish the regular season. They started 1–4, and the only win came against us. They just took it to us. When we walked off the field, we just said, "We're just not at that level yet."

We were just not prepared to go up against that defense. Warren Moon was great in that game. They ran the ball well. Houston had our number offensively. That game was ugly. But we watched the film and learned a lot from that game. We still didn't feel very comfortable going into the playoff game because we lacked any kind of success against their defense going in.

Part of Ryan's defense's aura was intimidation. The '85 Bears were intimidating, and Ryan brought that same intensity and intimidation to the Oilers. Leading up to the playoff game, he wasn't shy about shooting off his mouth. He shot off his mouth during the regular-season game, too. We noticed that he had a smirk on his face after plays. We weren't that much of a challenge, and he could pretty much have his way with us, so he felt pretty good about himself.

Ryan was not one to hold back. I actually love that about a coach. I really do. You'd better be able to back it up, and most of the time, Ryan could back it up. He was a big personality. He and head coach Kevin Gilbride got into a fistfight on the sideline earlier that year where they punched each other. Ryan was almost 60. He was really just a competitive, tough, nasty guy.

Being from Chicago, I knew all about him. In 1985 there were two teams: the Chicago Bears offense and the Chicago Bears defense. The same was true in Houston. There were the Houston Oilers offense and the Houston Oilers defense. Both of those defensive teams didn't like the offense. Usually, that doesn't work, but it had worked for them. He had issues with Bears coach Mike Ditka also. When the Bears won the Super Bowl, the offensive players carried Ditka off the field, and the defensive players carried Ryan off the field.

Before our playoff game, Ryan was talking about how Montana was washed up, and they were going to be able to put the pressure on Montana. We took it personally, but we kind of believed him. It, though, was motivation to kind of prove them wrong. We lost big time in the first game, and that's why certain things happened because the battle within the game was the Chiefs' offense against Ryan. It was more than the Chiefs' offense against Ryan's defense; it was us against Coach Ryan personally. We wanted to show him up because he took it to us, and it wasn't fun. The whole week before the playoff game, we talked about giving Montana some time against the defense, giving him opportunity to have success.

Football is different from a lot of other sports in that sometimes anger helps. In baseball if you see a pitcher throwing angry, he's not going to have control of his fastball. If you see a hitter hitting angry, he'll pop up or ground out. In football anger is a good motivating factor, as long as you can keep it under control. It's like the lesson from when my Notre Dame team played Miami. We were initially angry and we were motivated before Lou Holtz calmed us down, but it was a bad motivation. Had he not, we would've played on the outside of our game, and that was what Miami wanted. That was kind of what Ryan wanted, too.

One of things we talked about was that Ryan was going to get his. His defense was going to make plays. But we knew we had to keep going. We had to keep battling, keep hanging in there, and eventually something was going to show up, we were going to make a play, and we were going to figure it out. It was like watching *Wheel of Fortune*. There were all kinds of letters up there. We just couldn't see the answer. Then, all of a sudden, they flipped one square, and there it was. We'd know what the answer was. Once we figured it out, it was over. Joe threw three touchdown passes in the second half. Nobody did that against a Buddy Ryan defense.

Houston scored 10 in the first quarter, and nobody scored in the second quarter. We were down 10–0 at halftime, but we had that turning point I mentioned earlier. Right before halftime, Houston brought a six-man blitz. The Oilers brought both edges and one guy up the middle. They played a 3-4, and the three inside guys all came. We picked it up. Willie Davis went up the seam, and the ball tipped off Davis' hands for an incomplete pass. But we came into the locker room during halftime and looked at each other and said, "We've got it."

We had figured out how to pick up this blitz. That square flipped over, and we figured out the puzzle. We came out after the half, and they kept doing the same stuff because they were having success. They didn't think an incomplete pass would give us confidence, but it did. From that point on when they brought that pressure, we knew it was coming and we knew how to pick it up. We had the confidence to pick it up. If there's anything that you can get out of this book or anything out of watching the game of football, it's all about confidence. If you have confidence in what you're doing, if you believe in the guy next to you and you believe in the gameplan, you're going to have success. If you don't believe, you're going to hesitate. Any time you hesitate in the NFL, you lose. That's all it is. All the players are really good. Nobody is really that much better than the guys on the other side. But if you can get a guy to question things, maybe for just a half a second before the snap, he loses.

There's a famous video clip of Marty Schottenheimer talking to the offensive line on the sideline. He kept saying, "We've got it figured out. We've got to keep firing. We've got it figured out. We've got to focus."

We knew we had Montana, Marcus Allen, and guys who could get open on man-to-man coverage, and that is what they were playing. The rest of the game was easy. We made plays, scored touchdowns, and won the game 28–20. It really came back to an incomplete pass right before the half.

The most memorable score in that game didn't give us the lead. It was our first score of the game, our first score of any kind against Houston that season, and it came in the third quarter. Joe hit tight end Keith Cash in the flat, and he ran untouched into the end zone. That cut the score to 10–7. As I mentioned when I wrote about Cash in the last chapter, there was a big poster of Ryan in the end zone. The image of Ryan featured that obnoxious smirk. After Keith scored when he got to the corner of the endzone, he saw that poster, kind of looked back at the field, and then whipped the ball at Ryan's face on the poster. It broke the ice for us. It kind of slayed the dragon for us. Instead of throwing down the sword, he threw the football at the poster of Ryan in the end zone. (Just on a side note, Keith was a calm, cool, and collected guy. He wasn't a big trash talker. His reaction was completely against his personality, completely foreign from what he typically did.)

On the touchdown we picked up the blitz and gave Joe a little bit of time. They were usually flawless in that defense because they brought so much pressure. That touchdown didn't win the game. It didn't even give us the lead. It just cut the deficit to 10–7. Houston later had an 80-yard drive for a touchdown, and Ernest Givins caught a seven-yard touchdown pass to draw within 21–20, so we needed to go down and score to ice the victory.

That last touchdown was probably my favorite touchdown in my career. That's the time I said to Marcus in the huddle, "I'm just a fat kid from Chicago who never won anything. We've got to get this in the end zone, whatever it takes. Get on your blocks, finish your blocks. Marcus will get it in for us. Marcus will get it done. Give him a chance."

The funny thing was that I won a national championship at Notre Dame. But don't ever let the facts get in the way of a good story. I kept saying in the huddle, "Give him a chance. Give him a chance. Give him a chance."

We were at the 21-yard line. Marcus cut back against the grain. The run is still kind of in slow motion in my mind. That didn't happen a lot in my career, but it really just felt like that play was in slow motion. The nose tackle was slanting to the right. I got my head across and power-armed him off. Marcus was kind of where the hole was going to go, but he set it up so perfectly that he was able to go right behind my block. I saw his jersey just flash.

It was the best touchdown ever for me. We couldn't run the ball against those guys in the first game. We could barely run the ball against them in the second game. We finally figured out the pass protection and we were able to pass the ball. But in the red zone, you don't have as much space, and we had to find a way to run the ball. We knew it; they knew it. We had one of the best running backs in the NFL, a motivated offensive line, and a motivated huddle to get a touchdown.

As we were flying home after the game, the pilot said to us, "Look out the window. Your fans are here." The game was played in January, but there were thousands of people at the airport already standing outside the concourse. They were outside of their cars, cheering us on as we drove by. That was the coolest moment. We got our inspiration from the fans.

No. 1
Denver Broncos, 1994

We always struggled in Denver and were coming off a couple of losses after starting the season 3–0 in 1994. Even though the Denver Broncos came in 1–4, we knew it was a *Monday Night Football* matchup, a national TV matchup, a marquee game, the ultimate battle between two of the greatest quarterbacks of all time: John Elway and Joe Montana. People expected an unbelievable game, and they got their money's worth.

The contest went back and forth all game. It started out 7–7, then went to 14–14 at the half, then it was 21–21. It was a great matchup, a great battle between two great quarterbacks. With us up 24–21 in the fourth quarter, Denver fumbled the ball, but we went and fumbled it right back. I kind of take responsibility for that last fumble because I was blocking Ted Washington. He was 6'5" and 365 pounds, the biggest man in the NFL at that time. He just reached out that big ol' paw, which was about the size of a tennis racket, and hit the ball, and it came out. I felt responsible, but we went to the sideline confident the defense was going to stop them and we were going to win the game.

All of a sudden, "Elway magic" happened. It always happened. In the fourth quarter of every game that I remember playing against Elway, especially early in my career, the Broncos quarterback either threw for a touchdown, scrambled for a touchdown, or otherwise led a last-minute drive for a touchdown. Elway magic always reared its ugly head against the Chiefs.

He did it again in this game. The only difference was we knew we had the best of all time in those kinds of situations. We had Joe Cool, the two-minute master. He wrote the book on two-minute drives. We knew that we had him, but we were extremely nervous. I remember going into that huddle, and guys' eyes were wide open because we were nervous. But we knew if we gave Joe a clean pocket and gave him some time, he could pick apart any defense. There was nothing you could do defensively that he hadn't seen before, but we had to give him time. So as an offensive line we sat there and said, "This is our opportunity."

There was 1:29 left in the game when Elway scored. We had 1:22 after the kickoff and we had to go 75 yards. We were down by four. These were the situations you prepare for. We did it every week. Marty Schottenheimer would say, "We're down by four, there's 1:25 left, and we've got to go 80 yards." We practiced it and we practiced it and we practiced it.

Arrowhead Stadium is loud, extremely loud, but Denver is almost as loud. Mile High Stadium had very similar fans who had very, very similar attitudes and an understanding of the game. They're great fans out there, too. They were extremely loud, but I will tell you this: as nervous as we were going out there on that field, that fanbase was nervous because they knew that Joe Montana was going on the field.

We were out there on the field during the timeout. Joe was over there talking to Marty and offensive coordinator Paul Hackett. Nobody said a word in the huddle. It was not like, "Hey, let's get this thing going. We're going to go score here. We got this." Nobody was saying a word. It had that kind of intensity and nervousness to it.

Then Joe walked out, kind of like the cowboy walking down the dirt street in the old Western, kind of sauntering his way up to the huddle. We looked at him, and he looked at us. He said, "Hey, Grunny, did you see the chaps on the cheerleaders? How do they get away with wearing those out there?" I looked at him, and he said, "Relax, this is what I do."

That was a Montana thing. It was like his famous John Candy line at Super Bowl XXIII a few years before. He told us, "This is what we're going to do. Give me some time."

I've used this as a coach I can't tell you how many times. Joe said it himself. He said, "The team in orange is not our enemy. The down and distance is not our enemy. It's the clock. That's our enemy." He told the guys to get out of bounds after they caught the ball. He told the offensive linemen to get up to the line of scrimmage quickly. He said, "We've got to beat that enemy, and the enemy is the clock."

The o-line did a great job, and the wide receivers did a great job. There were no huge plays in that drive. It was all dink and dunk. Derrick Walker had a 12-yard catch. Walker was a great guy who played at Michigan, but he wasn't a pass-receiving tight end. Tracy Greene, another blocking tight end, had a 19-yard catch to set up first and goal with 13 seconds left. If you watch the video of the game on YouTube, you'll see how much time and space Joe had on the pass to Greene. There wasn't a defender within five yards when he threw the ball. He asked us to give him time, and we delivered. On the next play, Montana hit Willie Davis at the goal line. Davis stepped back across the goal line to make sure he had the touchdown. After the score *Monday Night Football* announcer Dan Dierdorf said, "Lord, You can take me now. I've seen it all."

The whole thing was synchronized by the best choreographer of all time in those situations—Joe. He hit Marcus Allen in the flat for five. He hit tight ends crossing the middle because Denver was playing deep. They were worried about the wide receivers. He hit a tight end that nobody even knew about or cared about in Greene. When I saw Greene rumbling and stumbling down the middle of the field with the ball in his hands like a loaf of bread, I was thinking, *Oh, my God, please go down, just go down.* He just kept running and running.

When we scored, Joe's wife was working for one of the TV stations, and she was on the sideline. After Joe celebrated with us, he went over and gave his wife a big hug and a kiss. I thought that was really cool. Here was a guy near the end of his career who has just orchestrated maybe one of the greatest drives ever on national TV in the final two minutes, and he was able to share a moment with his wife on the sideline. One of his daughters was on the field, too, and it was just so cool to see that. A moment within a moment. He was not only a great quarterback, but also a pretty cool husband and a great dad.

Standing on the sideline, it felt like a benchmark for a football season and a career. You have hurdles that you have to overcome. We got over the hurdle of winning a road playoff game earlier in Joe's time with us when we won in Houston. But we finally got over the hurdle of beating Denver at its own game. This was what the Broncos did. It seemed like with Elway that they always won, and we walked off the field feeling like we should have won, but we didn't.

This time it was different. As the clock wound down to 0:00, our guys were going crazy and crying and all that stuff. I remember being quiet and looking around. After all those years of preparation and sacrificing time to work on my craft as an NFL player, all the hurdles and all the different things that I had to deal with, it all just kind of felt like it was all worth it.

7

The Impact of
Marty Schottenheimer
and Carl Peterson

IT'S TIME TO TALK ABOUT THE MEN WHO WERE BEHIND CHIEFS Kingdom. Before Carl Peterson and Marty Schottenheimer arrived in Kansas City, Arrowhead Stadium was a ghost town. No one wanted to go to games. No one wanted to be associated with the franchise.

The year before I arrived in Kansas City, the Chiefs had a winning record for the first time since 1986, and that set the expectation for the future. It's no coincidence that the year before I arrived, Carl and Marty took over the team. If there's one phrase that summarizes what Marty was all about, it was: "outwork everybody."

His personality was formed not only by being born and raised in Pittsburgh, Pennsylvania, but also by outworking people in every aspect of his life. Whether it was playing high school football, playing college football, or playing in the pros, he had to work for every playing opportunity he got. After finishing his playing career in 1971, Marty got out of football and became a real estate agent.

At that point, he realized that if he ever got back into football as a coach, the team he coached would have to be okay with him doing it *his* way. If his way wasn't good enough, then he was just not going to do it. As an assistant coach, Marty always outworked everybody. His players were always the most physical and the most prepared. When he became a defensive coordinator, the same thing was true. When he became a head coach, his attitude did not change.

When a lot of people become head coaches, they think that because they're kind of the CEO that they have to take more of an oversight role, doing less hands-on coaching. Marty wasn't that way. He wanted to get dirty and coach. He always considered himself a teacher. He taught us to outwork everybody, not only in the classroom and in the weight room, but also on the football field in practice. His feeling was that would carry over into the games.

It was tough. Martyball was basically doing what other teams were not doing. We did 9-on-7, which is inside run-game practice, for 15 or 20 plays in each practice. We did that every day, and that included the day before games. We were out there in full pads and were working hard and doing all the things that most teams didn't do during the week. Marty was one of the forefathers of tough-minded coaches. We had one-on-one pass-blocking drills, we had one-on-one run-blocking drills. The linebackers and running backs practiced at full speed against each other. The wide receivers and defensive backs practiced full speed against each other. Practices were a grind. It was long and hard, but that's the only way he knew how to do it.

Instead of three yards and a cloud of dust, Martyball was creating that cloud of dust. And then when the dust cleared, you did it again. The mantra was to hit the other guy in the mouth at every opportunity. That was his attitude, but it came at a cost.

Marty was the head coach for 10 years in Kansas City, and the last nine were with me as the center. We went to the playoffs seven times in those nine years, but we only won postseason games in two of those seasons (1991 and 1993). There are plenty of people who think we peaked during the regular season because we were more prepared, but we ran out of gas in the playoffs. There might be some truth to that.

We worked hard and we put in a lot of effort, hours on the field and in the classroom, thinking that would equate into victories. But when we got to the playoffs, we hit that proverbial wall. I think guys were tired both mentally and physically. It really took something kind of special to dig deep to find that next gear in the playoffs. If the difference between the preseason games and the regular season games is an extra step, the playoffs are another step up, and we were never able to find that last gear. I think part of that was that the guys were so beat up and tired.

The big run that we made in the playoffs in 1993 with Joe Montana happened because Joe had a little bit of an effect on Marty with the San Francisco 49ers' attitude that he brought to the table. Maybe that year we were just a little bit fresher for the playoffs. But once Joe was gone, I think Marty pushed the gas again, and we went back to that attitude where we were going to outwork you and out-tough you.

In 1995 and 1997, we won our division with 13–3 records. Both years, we got beat at home in our first game. Since playoff football is just a little bit different than regular-season football, you have to find that extra gear, that extra step, that extra motor in the playoffs. I don't think we had that in the tank. Even though we won 13 games and we were at home—and that gave us the best opportunity to have success with all the internal enthusiasm and being in front of our home crowd—when you push the gas and there is nothing there, you just fall short.

I think we saw that in Marty his whole career. It wasn't just those seasons with 13–3 records. It wasn't just with the Chiefs.

It was basically all the teams that he coached. They were really good in the regular season, but when he got to the end, they just didn't have that extra juice to go. Marty only knew one way. I believe it was a successful way. I think Marty is a Hall of Fame coach, but I'm not sure he will ever get in the Hall of Fame because you're judged on Super Bowls and playoff wins, and he fell short when it came to that.

Prior to being the Chiefs' head coach, he led the Cleveland Browns to back-to-back AFC Championship Games, but both times they lost to the Denver Broncos. After leaving the Chiefs, being on ESPN for two seasons, and then one year coaching the Washington Redskins, he led the San Diego Chargers to 12–4 and 14–2 seasons. But both seasons ended with first-round upsets. It was the cross that Schottenheimer teams had to bear. We kind of cashed in our chips in the regular season in the hopes that we would score big or get a blackjack in the playoffs. The odds just weren't with us. We got to the playoffs because we kind of used all of our chips in the regular season.

I don't want to come across as negative with Marty. He saw something in me and made me a second-round NFL draft pick. He gave me my shot to start early in my rookie year and he always had my back. I learned a lot about toughness from him, even though I thought I was pretty tough with my background as the son of a Chicago police officer. And Marty's toughness came from playing college football at Pitt and being a linebacker in the AFL in the mid-1960s. He was an overachiever.

He was not particularly big for a pro football linebacker, but he had a pretty successful career because he just outworked everybody. That's how he had success as a coach as well. Those were the guys he was looking for on his team—no-nonsense overachievers. You look at all his drafts, and those were the guys he was looking for. He always had to have the guys who were the front center of the defense or the front center of the offense. Those were his guys. He wanted his personality to be reflected in those guys, and that's the way he drafted.

I was certainly a reach for him in the second round. I played guard in college, but he saw something in my attitude and in my toughness on and off the field, and that's what he wanted. He was trying to find that same intangible that he had. He said all the time, "I wasn't a very good athlete, but I was one of the smartest guys out there."

If you played for Marty, you had to be smart and put time and effort into the gameplan and to study it like he did. Those were the guys that he brought in. Defensive lineman Bill Maas and I used to fight almost every day in practice. Marty loved that toughness. I think I was a microcosm of the team. We were all in the same boat. Everybody worked hard. We would take the shuttle from Arrowhead up to the practice fields and then back after practice. Guys would fall asleep on the way back from the practice fields because they were just so exhausted from practice.

You would step across that threshold from the cement to the grass practice field and make a conscious effort of going to work because if you didn't go to work that day, you would be unable to hold on. The battles with Maas and with Neil Smith were part of the plan. I learned this a little bit at Notre Dame going against Chris Zorich. The game almost felt like a day off. The guys in practice would work us so hard that when we got to the game, I'd think, *This guy is no Neil Smith* or *This guy is no Dan Saleaumua.*

Marty would demand you to go all out in practice to be ready for the games. There was no taking it easy during practice. I'm not saying we didn't have fun. I'm not saying that we didn't enjoy being out there, but it certainly wasn't a walk in the park. We didn't know any better. Guys would come in from other teams, guys like Joe Montana or Marcus Allen, and they would say, "How do you do this? How do you do this all year round?" We didn't know any different.

People always ask, "How come you guys didn't win in the playoffs?" We didn't have an answer. We just thought we just didn't get it done. The offense didn't score enough, or the defense should have made some stops. But in retrospect, we were just so beat up and tired at the end. It was certainly a pattern. We were a reflection of our coach. Schottenheimer was a great man; he was a fair man. He made a point to be just as agitating on the offensive side as the defensive side and special teams, so it didn't feel like he was a defensive coach or an offensive coach or whatever. It felt like he was your coach, the coach of the team, and the guys played for that.

I'm sure people suggested to Marty that he was too tough on us during the season, which caused us to run out of gas in the playoffs, but Marty wasn't going to change. He was always going to be Marty Schottenheimer. He was going to coach the way he believed and he was going to teach the way he believed. We were going to do things as a reflection of our head coach. That would be like asking Bill Belichick to smile at a press conference. He isn't going to change. Training camp was going to be six weeks of hell when you're being coached by Marty. Our Wednesday, Thursday, and Friday would be three-hour practices in full pads, and we were going to go at it. We'd have Saturday to rest. We'd play on Sunday and be beaten up. We came in Monday and worked out and got treatment. Maybe we got to about 60 to 70 percent of feeling a little bit better. Tuesday was the day off, and we usually didn't do anything. We went at it Wednesday and kind of worked through it. On Thursday we went full speed. By the time Friday rolled around, we started to feel about 80 percent. If we were lucky, we got to about 90 percent by Saturday, and then it started all over again.

Much of the talk these days is about Andy Reid's success coming from his team's hard practices. Training camp is hard. The Chiefs practice hard during the week. But because of the collective bargaining agreement, NFL teams can't practice like we used to. What Andy does is practice harder than most other coaches, but it would be considered a vacation compared to the way we used to do it. If Andy could do some of the things he wanted to do, I'm sure that he would do them. The CBA says you can't tackle in practice. Training camp includes no two-a-days. Tackling in practice is a lot different. Blocking is totally different.

I coach high school football. You don't teach tackling by leading with your head. Your head is not even a part of the conversation. Everything back in the day was about getting your head across or "see what you hit and hit what you see." We were taught to throw our facemask in there on a tackle. It's all completely different now. It's better for the players.

The one thing that you didn't have to worry about with a Schottenheimer team was whether it was going to be physical enough for the game because we practiced physicality. In this day and age, Reid's teams have to tackle big physical running backs without much practice. Players don't tackle much in practice, and the starters see limited action in preseason games. The thing that Reid and Schottenheimer had in common: they both created competitive environments in practice.

In Marty's practices, we'd have Gunther Cunningham standing in the defensive huddle, jawing at the offense and the offense jawing back at him. Our two-minute situation practices were always a battle royale. Whichever team won, the other team would get upset. Those are the competitive situations, and the only difference is they don't tackle anymore. What are considered hard practices now would have been a day at the country club in my day.

But I think we needed those hard practices at that point. We were trying to connect with the fans, a blue-collar fanbase. They came out and spent their vacation money to come to Chiefs games. They wore their exuberance. They wanted to see a reflection of their community. Marty understood that because he came from Pittsburgh. That's how the Pittsburgh Steelers became the Pittsburgh Steelers. Don't mess with Steelers fans because they're tough.

Marty wanted that on the field so the fans could see it. The players cared about the game. The fans cared about the game. We gave them everything we possibly could on the field. They gave everything they had during the game. There was a symbiotic relationship between the Schottenheimer teams and the fans of the 1990s. The fans felt like they had something in common with the players on this team. They were the grinders, the tough, physical gladiators. It wasn't a California offense. It wasn't the run-and-shoot. It was Martyball. I'm going to pound you and pound you and pound you. That was an entertainment value for this city. Would it have worked in some other cities? Maybe not. But it worked here.

Marty had a side few people not on the team saw. But it was real. My very first conversation with Schottenheimer as a Chiefs player happened in Berlin, Germany, when we went to train against the Los Angeles Rams after a week or two weeks of training camp at William Jewell College. This was less than a year after the Berlin Wall, connecting East Germany and West Germany, fell. It was a great experience. We were practicing against the Rams. We were practicing on the old marching grounds where the Nazis had their evil parades right outside the stadium on a huge grass field.

It was my first time going against professional football players. It was hot and it was tough. After one of the practices, I got on the bus and sat in the back. I looked up, and here came Schottenheimer, and he sat right next to me. As close as I was with Lou Holtz late in my career, I can't ever remember sitting next to Holtz on the team bus. Marty sat down next to me and said, "Well, what do you think?"

I was thinking, *Okay, which way am I supposed to go with this?* I just said, "This is so cool being here in Germany. My relatives are German. I know you've got some relatives who are German, and the wall coming down, and this Olympic Stadium."

He said, "That's good, but what do you think about playing in the NFL? How do you think you're doing?"

At that point I was thinking I was in trouble because I always undersold myself. I always thought I wasn't doing as well as maybe I really was. I don't know how I came up with this answer, but it was the perfect answer. I said, "Marty, I think I'm really good at the stuff where I know what I'm doing. The things, where I question what I'm doing, I'm not where I need to be."

He said, "You're exactly right. I can tell when you're comfortable and doing the things where you know what you're doing that you look good. Then there are things that you're not quite sure of that you need to get a lot better." We had this conversation about football, and then he said this: "One of the reasons why we drafted you is that we knew you were smart and had that confidence and work ethic to get better. You need to combine those two. You've got to take that football smart and understanding and the study of football and combine it with that confidence because you can't have one without the other. You've got to have both if you're going to be right."

The bus ride was about 20 minutes back to the hotel. I thought it was really interesting that the head coach decided to come and sit next to me and kind of pick my brain to find out about how I thought I was playing. That was kind of cool. I knew Marty was different at that point. I kind of fell in love with Marty and I realized that this was the man I wanted to play for.

In October of my rookie year, my dad passed away right before Halloween. He was able to come to one Chiefs game before he died. My mom called me at my apartment right by the stadium and said, "Your father has taken a turn for the worse. You need to get down here." They were down in Mountain Home, Arkansas, at the time. That was where they retired.

I remember it was a Tuesday afternoon, which was the players' day off. I drove over to the stadium and walked up to Marty's office. I said, "Marty, my father has taken a turn for the worse, and I've got to get down there."

He said, "Where are you going to go?"

I said, "Mountain Home."

He said, "How long is that drive?"

I said, "It is probably about four and a half to five hours away."

He said, "In your mental state right now, I just don't want you to drive down there. Let me find a plane."

He called all the people he knew who had a plane but just couldn't find a plane to get me down there. The closest airport was Springfield, Missouri, and that really wouldn't have done me any good because I wouldn't have had a car. So we decided that I would drive, but he made me promise to check in with him frequently.

Then we talked for about an hour before I left. We talked about my dad. He said, "I'm sure he is proud of you." He talked about his father and his relationship with his father. After that, I got in the car and started driving. He told me, "I want you to call me when you get to Springfield and I want you to call me when you get to your parents' house in Mountain Home. I want you to call me every morning that you're there because I want an updated report."

I said, "Marty, I'm going to see my dad and I'm coming back. I'm not missing a game."

We were going to play against the Los Angeles Raiders, but he said, "Don't worry about the game. That will work itself out."

My father passed away on Thursday or Friday, so I didn't play in the game. But that was confirmation that Marty was the guy I want to play for. I'd run through walls for that guy. He cared. That was an important conversation for me. For the rest of my career, I had respect for that man. Whether he criticized or complimented me, whether he was mad or was excited about my play, I always knew that he had my back and that he was in my corner. It goes a long way when you're doing things that are uncomfortable or hard. It was an unbelievable feeling that I had for our relationship with each other.

The other phone call that I remember was when Derrick Thomas passed away. Marty called me. That was a very, very hard conversation. He called every single player. He didn't want anybody else to talk to the players but him. I was so blessed to have Marty in my life. I really only had four head coaches in my entire football career: my high school coach, Lou Holtz, Marty, and Gunther Cunningham. Lou and Marty were perfect coaches for me at the time when I needed them. I was so blessed, so lucky in my career.

It's funny. Lou and Marty were about as different as they could possibly be. Lou was a psychologist. He would find your weakness and exploit it. Marty would demand excellence and toughness from you, but he would expect that from himself also. He led by example—not that Lou didn't lead by example. What I'm saying is Marty had a way of getting the most out of his players, and he didn't have to ask twice. You just looked at the way he was working, putting in 18, 19 hours. You'd see him giving a presentation to the team when he was exhausted. You knew this guy was all in, and we had to be that way, too.

I mentioned previously that Lou knew which buttons to push. He knew that I was a pleaser and he didn't want me getting to be comfortable, so he was always dangling that carrot in front of me. Marty actually would call me in and tell me, "We need you to lead this team and this offense. You've got to have this personality."

The quarterback is a better voice, but at times that was a revolving door, and the quarterback either couldn't do it or hadn't earned the credibility in their career in town to be able to do that. So the common denominator was me. He entrusted that to me, so I kind of switched from trying to please to trying to lead. I took my motivation from college, where I tried to please the coach and to show him I was good enough to play in the NFL, to the Chiefs, where it was about leading the team, getting out front, getting my teammates to work hard in practice, and communicating to make sure they were doing their best. That was kind of how I filled that void.

Marty didn't do a lot of joking around, but I do remember one funny moment with him. I had just signed my rookie contract and I was in the locker room. I had just bought a house in Lee's Summit. I can't remember who I was talking to, but I said, "I just bought a house. I'm getting ready to move out there, leaving the apartment to move into a house."

Marty must have heard that. He stopped in his tracks, turned around, and said, "What did you say? You bought a house?"

I said, "Yeah, I bought a house in Lee's Summit. I think Dave Szott is going to move in with me. We're going to get out of that apartment."

He said, "Are you sure you ought to buy that house?"

I said, "Sure, it's a nice house, I got a pretty good deal on it. I got some land, which is what I always wanted. In Chicago I could reach out the window and touch the house next door. I always wanted to have space."

He said, "No, that's not what I mean. How do you know you're even going to be here next year?"

He could tell from my face that I was devastated. He said, "I'm only kidding. You're going to be here longer than I'm going to be here."

But it made me think twice about the whole thing. When he walked away and said that he was kidding, that was still in the back of my mind. *Was he serious?* Schottenheimer had what we called the "camp personality." The camp personality was part stern, tough grinder, and then later you'd see him messing around with the coaching staff and having a beer. You never were quite sure which one you were going to get.

On the field it was always the same. It was always this tough grinder. It was weird. We wondered which Schottenheimer was going to show up each year. Was it going to be the guy who is going to be relaxed and let his hair down, or was it the guy with his nose to the grindstone every second in camp? It changed. It changed from camp to camp. It changed from year to year. It was an enigma in itself, regarding which Schottenheimer was going to show up.

I think Marty doesn't get the credit he deserves because he was unable to reach a Super Bowl. In the decade of the 1990s, the Chiefs won more than 100 games. Marty was an excellent coach. He only knew one speed. It may have affected our performance in the playoffs and not reaching the Super Bowl, but he certainly should be in the Hall of Fame as a coach. He got the best out of his players and won a lot of football games.

Of course, Marty and Carl came to the Chiefs together. Carl was hired first, and his first hire was Marty. They were joined at the hip. Carl lasted longer than Marty, but I believe that when most people think of one of them, they also think of the other. Like it was with Marty, Carl ultimate goal was to win a Super Bowl. Anything less than that was not successful for him. It's just like the players. Your goal is to go win a Super Bowl. Carl deserves a lot of credit once again with the rebirth of the Kingdom and for getting the fans and the right players in place.

I thought there were times in his career when he reached a little bit too far with some of the players he brought in. He overlooked some flaws because of their talent, and that backfired. The Chiefs took chances on people they probably shouldn't have taken chances on. I don't want to name those people, but there were some guys that he brought in who were just not good guys. He did it with the idea that we were just one piece away or one player away from getting where we needed to go.

To be fair, there were far more times when he brought in players like Joe Montana, Marcus Allen, or Rich Gannon. He brought in some quarterbacks who had some success. Over the 20 years that Marty was there, he made some really good decisions. I think he probably made some decisions that he regretted, but I don't think he gets enough credit for the successes that he had. He was the foreman of the foundation for Chiefs Kingdom. I don't think anybody could take that away from him. Maybe it would be better to say that Marty was the foreman, but Carl was the architect. The players were the laborers.

Carl had a plan and he stuck with his plan. He was good with management. He got along great with the Hunt family. He and Lamar Hunt had a very close relationship. I'm not sure about the relationship Carl had with Clark, but Lamar had a very good relationship with him. Carl hired people who understood what was required to put together a successful organization. That included president Denny Thum and Tim Conley, who was basically an assistant vice president. Conley worked for a telecom company before coming to the Chiefs. He brought the ideas of the corporate world into football.

Carl did a really good job of taking the Chiefs into the 21st century. Jack Steadman was a great guy and a good football person, but Carl took the Chiefs out of that approach of just playing football on the field to taking advantage of what the NFL is all about. Steadman was part of the franchise when it came to Kansas City in 1963 and he had a lot of success. It didn't end well from an on-field standpoint, but Carl had some big shoes to fill in terms of being the CEO of the company. He had the personality to say, "Bring it on."

He had that brash, confident personality. He knew the game of football. He was a coach before he became an executive. As an executive for the Philadelphia Stars of the USFL, he had a lot of success winning two championships in the three-year history of the league. Lamar Hunt saw that the NFL was passing him by, and his team was falling behind. He knew that he needed to bring in a new front office to get with the times for better or for worse.

I thought Carl did a nice job of including the past players and building a relationship with the current players. That was very, very unusual. I think he wanted to connect to the tradition of the Chiefs and let the younger guys understand that tradition is important. His relationship with the past players coincided with his relationship with the fans. He understood the role the past players could play and he started the Chiefs Ambassadors. He understood the role the fans could play and that the four-prong entity of the Chiefs included the front office, the players, the coaches, and the fans.

Peterson had an interesting philosophy in his time as an executive. He may have been one of the forefathers of this theory, though a lot of teams use it today. I call it "Stars and JAGs." We all know what we mean by stars; JAGs is an acronym for "Just Another Guy." Obviously, these JAGs have a lot of athletic and football ability. The fact that they were able to make an NFL roster means they were the cream of the crop. But they weren't the cream of the cream of the crop. With the Chiefs he had stars on the defensive side with Derrick Thomas and Neil Smith. When we finally got over the hump and started winning playoff games, it was with the stars of stars—Joe Montana and Marcus Allen on the offense. Even though those guys might have been at the tail end of their careers and past the peak of their athletic abilities, they were still stars and knew how to win. Carl recognized the value of that.

Very few offensive linemen are stars. We had one of the best offensive lines in the NFL, but that was as a unit. We needed each other; individually, we were not the players you built championships around. Carl wanted to surround himself with people who knew how to win. And whether that was a guy who was a little bit older or who may have caused some issues, he would take chances because he wanted winners around him and around the team.

That's why when Montana and Allen became available, he went after them. Yeah, they might have been a little bit older, but you can't teach experience. You can't share that knowledge without having the experience to do it. Carl understood that. Sometimes general managers are a little bit nervous about bringing in big personalities, but he wasn't afraid to do that, whether it was the star of stars or it was a big guy with a big personality who would speak his mind. You've got to give a lot of credit to Carl because even with Carl and Marty there was a love/hate relationship. There were times when they didn't like each other. There were times when they loved each other. But they were able to work together no matter what.

After the 1988 season, Lamar Hunt didn't announce that he was cleaning house, but it was pretty obvious that he was going to do that. He hired Carl and phased out Steadman. He said it would be up to Carl whether to keep the current coach—Frank Gansz—or to hire his own coach. Fortunately for Chiefs fans, Carl made the right choice. Carl and Marty let each other have their own personalities. They let each other stay in their own lanes. I don't think that Marty stepped into Carl's lane very often and I don't think that Carl stepped into Marty's lane too much, which is very unusual. Since they were big, type-A personalities, you could tell when they did step into the other's lane. When Marty stepped into Carl's domain, they didn't mince words; they didn't get along. When Carl stepped into Marty's domain, the same thing happened. So they basically stayed in their own lanes because they knew the trouble that not doing so would cause.

There were times—like any relationship that lasts 10 years—that maybe they didn't see eye-to-eye on things, but most of the time, they were able to work together because they respected each other. They respected each other's knowledge and work ethic and they knew that each other had the best in mind for the team.

While Marty was a football man, Carl was a company man. He was going to do the best that he could possibly do for his owner and his organization. He was a tough negotiator. When guys were free agents or when they were holding out, they'd be called up into the suite. They would sit in the suite with Carl during preseason games, and the next thing you knew, they would be signing the next day. We'd say, "Carl's got him in the box, so he'll be signing."

That was kind of his spider web up there, where he'd get you in his clutches and he'd get it taken care of. Not only did we know it inside the locker room, but the fans also knew it. If there was a player holding out and they saw him on TV in the box with Peterson during a preseason game, they could rest assured that that guy would be in training camp or at practice the next day.

He did a really good job of holding the best interest of the club in mind; sometimes it was to the detriment of the player. But to be really honest with you, I think he was a very loyal guy to his players, maybe almost to a fault. When maybe a guy

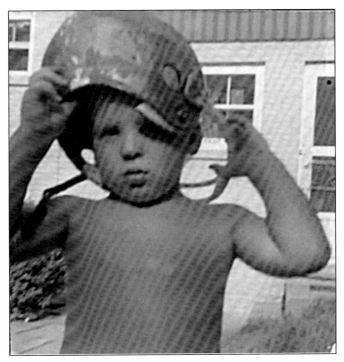

I was destined to be a Kansas City Chiefs player because it was the first helmet I received when I was just three years old. My dad spray painted it gold for Notre Dame, but the Chiefs colors still seeped through. (Tim Grunhard)

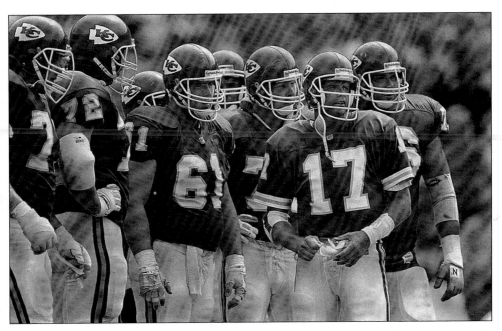

Quarterback Steve DeBerg (No. 17) had the perfect demeanor to lead the Chiefs as we transitioned from the disappointing 1980s to the playoff teams of the 1990s. (Kansas City Chiefs)

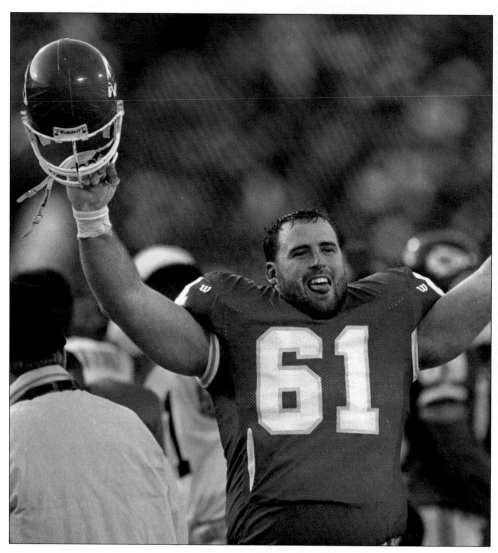

I celebrate my second playoff victory after defeating the Pittsburgh Steelers in overtime, following the 1993 season. (Kansas City Chiefs)

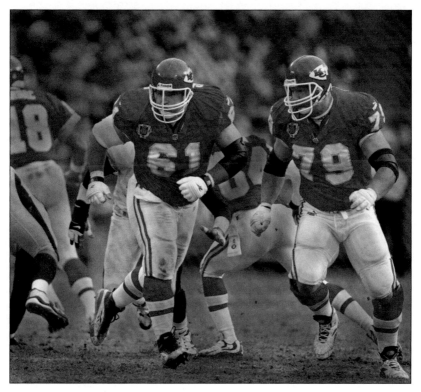

I block with my good pal, linemate, and former roommate Dave Szott during a win against the Pittsburgh Steelers in 1999. (Kansas City Chiefs)

I meet with the rest of the captains for the coin toss of an overtime loss at the Tennessee Titans during 2000, my last year in the NFL. (Kansas City Chiefs)

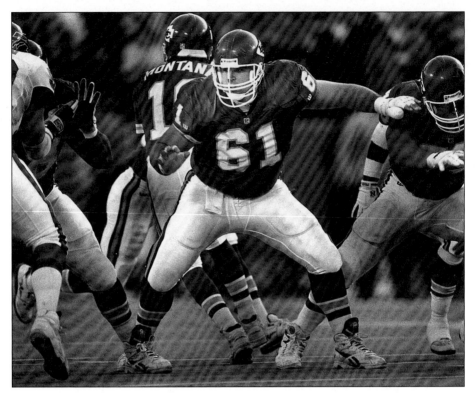

Snapping to and blocking for Joe Montana, one of the best quarterbacks ever, was the ultimate. (Kansas City Chiefs)

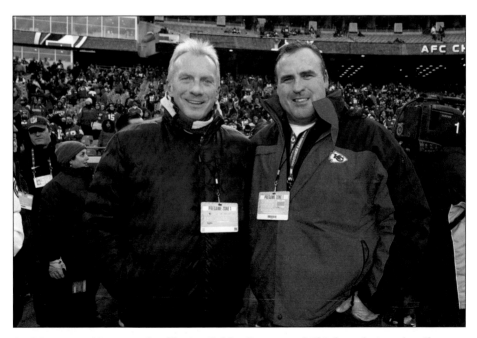

Joe Montana and I—a couple of former Golden Domers and Chiefs—take in a playoff game at Arrowhead Stadium. (Kansas City Chiefs)

My family and the general manager who drafted me, Carl Peterson, pose with my Chiefs Hall of Fame bust. Through the eyes of the bust, I could see the struggle, emotion, pride, and love of the game. (Kansas City Chiefs)

Chiefs owner Clark Hunt presents me with my jersey while inducting me into the Chiefs Hall of Fame during the 2021 season. (Kansas City Chiefs)

During the *Monday Night Football* game against the New York Giants, I prepare to bang the ceremonial drum. (Kansas City Chiefs)

I bring the same kind of intensity to banging the Chiefs drum that I used to bring while playing for the Chiefs. (Kansas City Chiefs)

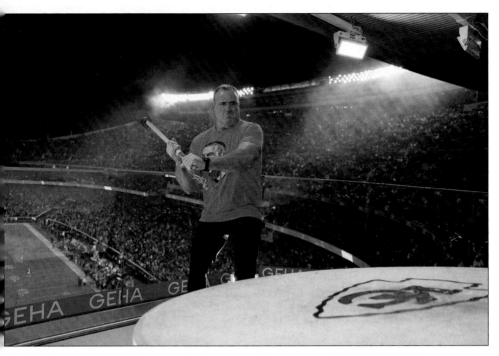

I let out the emotions while banging the drum. My induction into the Chiefs Hall of Fame was a goal I articulated to Carl Peterson when he drafted me. (Kansas City Chiefs)

Having the sellout crowd of Arrowhead Stadium cheer me on while I banged the drum gave me goose bumps like back in my playing days. (Kansas City Chiefs)

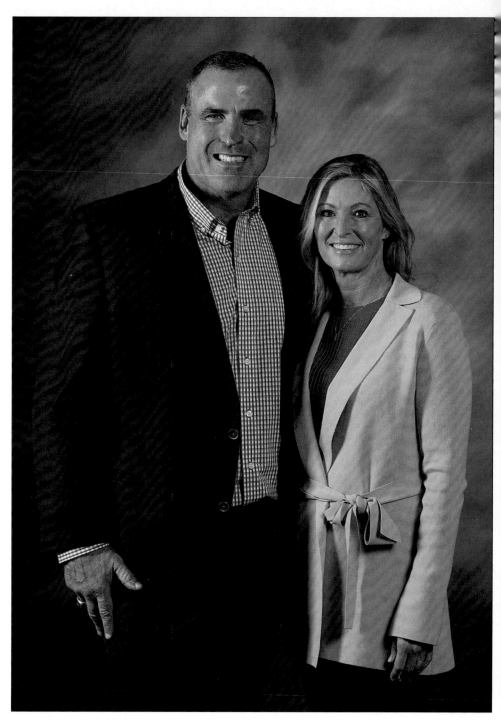

Sarah, whom I met as a freshman at Notre Dame, remains my rock to this day. (Kansas City Chiefs)

should have been let go, he would give them another year or two. A lot of people gave him flack for that because he was just so loyal to the guys.

Carl's specialty was finding talent that others didn't. That's why Plan B free agency worked so well for him. He was a great evaluator of talent. Carl and Marty did really a good job of understanding what the team needed. Carl understood what Marty wanted in a player, and Marty understood what Carl needed as far as his system. Marty would take care of the Xs and Os, and Carl was really good at bringing him the Jimmys and Joes. The Jimmys and Joes had to fit those Xs and Os for that team to win. Carl was really good at doing that. Many times it wasn't the biggest name guy, but it was the guy who fit in that system the best.

The player also had to have the right attitude. Like the guy who challenged me in the Oklahoma drill during training camp in my rookie year, calling attention to yourself without merit was not a good thing to either Carl or Marty. You'd better earn that merit. You'd better earn that badge on your chest because nobody is going to give it to you.

One of the players who earned the respect was Derrick. DT and Carl had a special relationship. Maybe it was because Derrick was Carl's first draft pick, but they were really tight. There was never any animosity from the other players about that relationship. Derrick and Carl had almost a father-and-son relationship. Derrick didn't have that father figure in his life when he was drafted by Chiefs because his dad died during the Vietnam War.

Carl—and Bill Cowher—stood on the table to draft Derrick. So maybe that's another reason Carl was drawn to him. When Derrick got to Kansas City, Carl took him under his wing for both on-the-field and off-the-field stuff, making sure that he was not making decisions that were detrimental to him. Derrick obviously made a lot of those, but Carl tried as much as he could to constantly counsel Derrick. They would go out to dinner almost weekly. Carl regularly had Derrick over to his house. They had a really good relationship, where it was very comfortable for both of them. We'd always say to Derrick, "Your Daddy's here. Go see your Daddy."

It wasn't derogatory; nobody looked at it like Derrick was getting special treatment. It was just a fact. Derrick was hard on himself and he had a tendency to pout a little bit if he wasn't performing. Carl was the only one who could get him out of that. Marty would attempt it and at times he probably had a little bit of success. But Carl was the one who could get Derrick out of his funk. He could get the best out of Derrick.

When Derrick passed away, it was like losing a son for Carl. It was like losing a brother for us, but I think when Derrick passed away, Carl lost some of his love of the Chiefs. It's not like he wasn't happy or didn't care. But I think when he looked out on the field, he fed off of No. 58 being out there. When he wasn't out there, it affected Carl personally. He wasn't the same for the years that he was with the Chiefs after that. I think Derrick was a big part of why Carl loved the Chiefs organization.

Like every human being, there was a funny side to Carl, who was famous for leaving for vacation three weeks before training camp started. If you were negotiating a contract, he would not only tell you, but he also would tell your agent, "Hey, listen, we need to get this done because I'm going to be gone."

That was his plan to just kind of force the issue to get it done. If you didn't have a contract three weeks before camp started, you were probably going to miss some of training camp.

He'd say, "We'll have to start negotiating once the season starts." Nobody wanted that because if you miss regular-season games, you'd miss paychecks.

I got called up to his office late in June when I was a rookie. I thought that I was pretty smart and that I understood the business world. I came from Notre Dame and I felt like I was intelligent. So I was up there just talking, and all of a sudden, contract talks start to come up. He said, "You know what? We need to get this done early. It's going to hurt you if you're not ready for training camp."

He was kind of putting the pressure on me. We were going back and forth with numbers. I thought I was doing a great job. I could do this agent stuff. It was no big deal. After about two hours of us going back and forth, I felt like we had something. I called my agent. He was pretty upset. "Why are you up there negotiating your contract with Carl Peterson? That's my job. Let me talk to Carl."

Carl got on the phone and he was like the cat that ate the canary. He said, "We've got a contract here. Tim is comfortable with it. I'm comfortable with it and I think this is what we're going to go with."

My agent got me back on the phone and said, "Walk out of there."

I was embarrassed. It was really kind of a sucker job. Carl brought me in there and got this contract done, which was basically what he wanted. As I started to leave, Carl said, "Well, if you leave, I want you to know that I'm not going to be negotiating in the next couple of days."

My agent called him back and basically worked it out. I think he got me a couple of extra dollars here and there, and we signed the contract. But my agent said, "Never go in and negotiate your own contract."

It was funny because Carl took advantage of a guy with a little bit of ego and a little bit of knowledge. That was Carl. He was going to take care of his owner and his team first. The rest of my time with the Chiefs, I never talked to him about contracts again.

The other funny story about Carl happened after the "Monday Night Meltdown." Once again it was about Derrick. DT got three personal fouls on one drive. It was absolutely the lowest point in Derrick's career, and the Chiefs suspended him for a game. After that game Lamar Hunt was not happy. That's the only time I ever saw Lamar come into the locker room in a bad mood. He yelled and screamed at us as much as Lamar could yell and scream. Lamar was the kind of person who would be that grandfatherly person even after a loss. He'd tap you on the shoulder and say, "We'll get them next time. Don't worry about it."

The next time we were together was at Wednesday practice. After practice was done, Carl came storming out on the field. We were called together at the end of practice as Marty was talking about the meltdown. He said, "We've got to be better than that. We can't let other teams get under our skin. We represent the Kansas City Chiefs and the Hunt family."

Carl came out all disheveled. His tie was loose. His hair, which was always perfect, was everywhere. He must have just gotten out of a meeting with Lamar. He got the message: you can do whatever you want, but don't embarrass the Hunt family. If you make a mistake, own up to it and apologize. But if you make a mistake and you lie, you're not going to be there very long. There are a bunch of examples both in my era and even recently that I won't mention.

Carl got that "Don't embarrass the Hunt family" speech from Lamar right before that. So he came running out on the field and was just giving it to us. No one wanted to look directly at him probably for fear of being addressed personally. I looked down, and Carl had two different shoes on. He had a wingtip on the right foot and a penny loafer on the other. I turned over to Dave Szott and said, "Look at his shoes."

Dave started that laugh like when you're in church and you're not really supposed to be laughing but can't control it. Carl was just glaring at both of us. We were trying not to laugh anymore, but other people started picking up on it. Years later, I told him that he had two different shoes on when he came out to address us after that situation. He laughed and giggled about it.

I've spent a lot of pages in this chapter talking about Marty and Carl because they were so much a part of my career and especially the rebirth of the Chiefs Kingdom. But I would be remiss if I didn't talk about some of the other coaches who were part of that regime, especially Gunther.

When Marty was the head coach, Gunther was the defensive coordinator. He was also the juice of the team. He brought energy. He brought enthusiasm. He brought toughness. He brought intensity to practice. He did a really good job of getting his defensive players ready for a practice and goading the offensive players into playing hard against the defense. I loved that, as I was kind of the same personality on the offensive side, talking smack back to Gunther and to the defense. To get the best out of practice, we had to get the juices flowing and we did. It was fun. He would dial up all kinds of blitzes and try to do all kinds of different things to test us. If we had success against his defense, we wouldn't go over and say something to the players. We'd say something to Gunther in order to get under his skin.

Gunther brought a high amount of intensity. He grew up in Germany in the shadows of the Berlin Wall. He didn't speak much English when he came over to the United States as a German after World War II. Football was his release. It was his escape, and he loved the game of football because football saved him. That's kind of what he brought to the Chiefs. When they hired Gunther, we just kind of hit it off with very similar personalities.

That same approach didn't work when he was head coach. It would have worked, but Gunther could not delegate. He burned himself out. Gunther would start work at 6:00 AM and wouldn't end until 3:00 AM. It wasn't just the Xs and Os. He would set up the seating chart on the plane. He would set up the wives' parking situation for game days. He would worry about the dinner we would have after the game. He would take care of all these different things that just would burn him out. He would do little things like that instead of just sticking with what he was good at and that was football.

Gunther was famous for respecting the game. He would tell us constantly, "Respect the shield of the NFL and respect the game." To him that meant we didn't take our helmets off during practice. We also never sat down during practice. During water breaks we got water, but we didn't sit down. The worst thing we could do was take our helmet off *and sit down on it.* When that would happen, he would stop the practice, whistle, and just ream whoever was doing that. He was as old school as it gets.

We were in the middle of a practice one time, and he stopped the practice and blew the whistle. He said, "Hey, you down there. Get up off that bag."

Len Dawson jumped up, and Gunther, realizing it was Dawson, said, "You can sit down over there. Don't worry about it."

Lenny said, "Oh, no, rules are rules."

Another thing that was humorous about Gunther was that he was famous for being a soft talker, like the character on *Seinfeld*. When we traveled to away games, the offense would sit on one side of the plane, and the defense would sit on the other. Many times, I found myself sitting across the aisle from Cunningham, who would always start the conversation talking really loudly. But by the end of it, I would have to lean in, stick my ear in there because it would get quieter and quieter and quieter. We used to call him the soft talker. At first, I would have to lean away from him because he was talking so loud, and by the end of it, I would have to lean in to hear what he was saying. I don't know why he did that. There must have been some sort of technique because everything he did was with a purpose.

Gunther was not a conversationalist. He was funny during his press conferences. He would have some great quirky quotes. His famous quote was: "We're going to go after that running back. First, we're going to take away the heart of that team and knock that running back out of the game. Then, we're going to go after the soul of the team, and that's their quarterback."

When he was the defensive coordinator under Schottenheimer, we'd have team meetings, and they would pull the divider across with the defense on one side and the offense on one side. I would sit purposely with my ear against the divider so I could listen to Gunther because I knew he was going to get those guys going and get juiced up. I loved listening to him talk about how we're going to take their soul away, we're going to hit them in the mouth. It was old school, tough, hard-nosed football.

I think if Gunther had had a couple more years as a head coach, he could have been really successful when he figured out he didn't have to do everything. As it was, he had a .500 record. He would have gotten better and better.

I need to mention Howard Mudd. He was a Renaissance man. He was way ahead of his time as far as social issues. He rode his motorcycle everywhere. He was kind of the Peter Fonda of coaching. He was *Easy Rider*. If you asked him a question, he would sit back, take his glasses off, stare up into space maybe 20 or 30 seconds, and then answer the question. That's just the way he was. He used to say to us all the time, "I know you better than you know you." We didn't know what he was talking about. He would follow that with, "I know what you can do. I know where you can go. I know what kind of player you can be—even if you don't know what you can be."

He would test you. He would goad you and embarrass you and he would get in your face until you stood up to him. Then he would laugh and say, "Fight me." He wanted to test you to see how tough you could be and how much you could take.

Bill Cowher was another great coach for us, but he was a defensive coach, so he never coached me. But we got along really well and related well to each other. Bill and I only spent one year together. We had a really good relationship because we sat right next to each other in the team meeting room for some reason. We would be watching a film, and Marty would be going over the opposing offense or the defense and watching film on each one. At the end of it, Bill would say to me, "Okay, who have you got? You've got one pick, one draft pick on the team we're playing today. Who have you got?"

I'd say, "Reggie White" or "I'll take Dan Marino."

It was the same kind of relationship I had with Gunther. I tried to be the kind of personality and the juice of the offense, and Bill was that for the defense almost to a fault. He was the frenzied kind of coach. But even though we were on the same team for just one season, to this day we give each other a big hug and say "I love you" when we see each other.

One year we were playing against the Steelers when Bill was Pittsburgh's head coach and Gunther was our head coach. Like I always did before we played Pittsburgh, I found Bill and gave him a big hug. We chatted for a few minutes and then we gave each other a big hug and walked off. Gunther took a picture of it. The next day, he put the picture up on the big screen of me hugging Bill to make fun of me. To this day, if I have something going on, Bill is always one of the people I speak with because I value his opinion.

Tony Dungy was another defensive coach who impacted me in a short period of time. Tony was about as far away from me as you possibly could be. I was an offensive lineman, and he was the defensive backs coach. He was always in the defensive room, and I was in the offensive room. But we had this weird relationship. He was a historian of football. He knew the NFL and knew all the players. That was one of the things I prided myself on, especially Chicago guys. So when we would run sprints, Dungy was on one end of the run. He would say, "No. 35, Chicago Bears, 1980?"

I would say, "Roland Harper."

The next time down, he would say, "No. 73 of the offensive line in the Super Bowl?"

I would say, "Mike Hartenstine."

He would say, "You got it."

I loved what he used to say at the end of team meetings. He'd say, "Sleep fast. It's going to be here before you know it. We're starting all over again."

He was a fun guy to be around, a really smart person, a really genuine person. He would kill you with kindness. In this day and age of coaches who scream and yell, he had a quiet resolve to him. He wasn't a big yeller. He wasn't a guy who would draw attention to himself. There are a lot of coaches out there who draw attention to themselves. They want to show how good a coach they are by screaming at the players. Tony was the opposite of that. When he was working with Dale Carter or anybody, he was hugging them and drawing them in close and whispering in their ears. He would never embarrass players out loud. I respected that about Tony. I always thought he was a coach who got it. He understood the player. He understood the game. He understood the psychology of it.

A lot of times when you embarrass or scream at somebody, they'll turn you off. That's one thing that never happened with Tony. They never turned Tony off. That's why he became such a successful coach. If you follow him on social media, you know he is a great family man. He has a great perspective on life and the game. You've got to respect that kind of person.

Paying It Back

I HAD A LENGTHY PRO FOOTBALL CAREER, CONSIDERING THE average NFL career is less than 3.5 years. If you count my four years at Notre Dame and four years at St. Laurence High School in Chicago, I played organized football for 19 years. But I've been retired for more years than I played. That's hard to believe, especially since there are some mornings when I wake up feeling like I played the night before.

But I've had plenty of time to be involved in things other than playing football. All of them are related to the Chiefs Kingdom. Some of the things I'm involved in to this day began when I wore Chiefs red and gold. Others began after my career ended. One of the first things I did after becoming a Kansas City Chiefs player was to lend my name and time to a new initiative called First Downs for Down Syndrome. The Down Syndrome Guild was looking for some Chiefs representatives to be involved. The Arizona Cardinals tried something to promote awareness of Down syndrome in the late 1980s, but it wasn't really successful. Local television personality Gordon Docking welcomed a baby with Down syndrome and noticed that there were no support organizations for those families in the Kansas City area.

Gordon set out to change that. He thought it would be a great fit with our offensive line because raising a child with Down syndrome is a grind, kind of like being an offense lineman. Maybe since I was fairly new with the Chiefs, he thought the organization could grow with me and my career. That's when Gordon went to Brenda Snezik, who was our community relations person and asked if I'd like to get involved.

It was a perfect fit for the offensive line. The quarterbacks and the skill position players were all about scoring points. But without first downs, they'd only have three chances each possession. The goal of the offensive line was to move the defense so that first downs would keep drives alive. The concept of first downs for Down syndrome made sense because you're not going to have the big play in life with a child with Down syndrome. It's all about continuing to move the line of scrimmage forward.

When they came to me, I was thrilled to help them because I had a first cousin with Down syndrome. I was very, very close to him. His name was Peter. I spent my whole life going to family parties and having Peter come over to our house. He was probably about 15 years older than I was and he was kind of my little guardian angel. When the kids would pick on me, he would go over and stick up for me. I thought that was really cool, and we had a really nice relationship. There were many times when he came to Notre Dame games, and I'd walk him down the tunnel. He would just be thrilled.

So, this was a natural progression for me. I felt very comfortable being around people with Down syndrome and I wanted to help. I saw the challenges and I saw the different hurdles that Peter had to go through. I wanted to be able to help people here in Kansas City who were going through the process. The very first time Gordon came, he brought four or five kids with Down syndrome, including his son, Blake. We fell in love with those kids. They were in different stages in their lives. Some of the kids came periodically, but there were several of them who were always there. We got to hang out with them on the field and throw the ball to them and do all those kinds of things. We became pretty close to those kids.

It was really important to me and the rest of the offensive line. That was our group, and we did things with them. The offensive line is like a hand. You have the five individual units, but the hand is strongest when you make a fist, when you all come together. We wanted to show that same concept in charitable work, so it was a great fit. We had the Down Syndrome Walk every year. We had Christmas parties every year.

Along the walls of the stadium surrounding the field were all the posters of all the different charitable works the guys were doing. Some of them were really cool, and some of them were very basic. It showed not only the Kansas City community, but also the nation how involved the Chiefs were in the community.

That was a part of a conscious effort by Carl Peterson and Marty Schottenheimer to get players involved in the community to build those relationships so that they could become a part of the fabric of the Chiefs Kingdom. Since I was in love with the kids involved in the program, it tied perfectly in with the fact that Carl and Marty wanted the community to fall in love with Chiefs players.

I don't mean to overgeneralize, but people with Down syndrome have a beautiful perspective on life that exudes love and caring. When people find out they have a child with Down syndrome, the first reaction is that it's going to be a burden and a problem. Then they realize that it's a gift. Those kids are the closest thing to angels that you can be around. They are just full of love and they love life. If we all could take a page from those kids and let our emotions be shown and react with the honesty that they do, this world would be so much better.

Often I get credited for doing something special by lending my name and a lot of my time to First Downs for Down Syndrome. But that's the opposite of the truth. It was such a benefit to the members of the offensive line. We wanted to give back and wanted to be a part of the fabric of the community. Every time those kids came around, it was like moths to a light. All the guys wanted to be a part of it. There was a special feeling that you got when you were around those kids. I think it reminded us all of how blessed we were to be in the position where we could help but also to be around these kids and learn to enjoy life.

What better group could the offensive line learn from? Enjoy the challenge. Embrace the newness of a new defense, a new play, or a new experience. We learned that from those kids. Everything that they did, they did with a purpose and a passion. That was a great example. Those kids were eight, nine, 10, 11 years old. You would think that we were their role models, but it was the other way around. They were our role models. We learned a lot from them.

Another way I wanted to pay it back was by getting into coaching. The very first year after retiring, I was burned out. That was after the 2000 season. I got into radio and I was excited about staying involved, but I was burned out on football. Ken Kremer, who was a Chiefs Ambassador and was also part of my agent's group, was very involved with St. Pius High School. Rick Byers was the head coach at St. Pius and he had a football camp in the summer. I actually started doing his camp as a player in 1992, so it was a natural progression.

I realized pretty quickly—even that fall—how much I missed the day-to-day part of football. The next year he asked me again, and I said yes. In 2001 I started coaching at St. Pius High and just loved it. I loved being able to share my experiences and my knowledge of the game. I understood that I could make a difference in kids' lives at the high-school level probably more than at any other level because a lot of those kids were going through some transitions in life that were challenges for them.

I always believed football was a microcosm of life. In every situation in life, you've got to find a way to convert. If things are going badly, you've got to change the momentum. There are a lot of fourth-down situations in life. Those are some of the lessons that I thought I could pass on to these young kids. I told Byers halfway through that season that it really saved me because it gave me back a love of the sport. Being able to coach those kids—and we won a state championship—was great. It really was kind of a rebirth for me. It was another career. I knew at that point that that was what I wanted to do.

I could have gone on and been a TV analyst. I'd been offered that before, but I would have had to give up working with kids and giving kids an opportunity to use football. I always tell the kids to use football as a vehicle to experience different things, maybe even use it as a chance to go to college or even a chance to be a professional athlete. I wouldn't have had that opportunity if I would have been traveling and doing games on television or radio. That was more important to me because, as Herm Edwards used to say, "You've got to coach on the dirt in order to understand the game." And Herm was right. You've got to coach on the dirt.

My coaching career has been a winding road. From 2001 to 2005, I was at St. Pius as the offensive line coach. At that point I received a call from someone over at Bishop Miege High School who said they needed a head coach. I called the president of the school and left a message on his phone saying, "I'm interested."

The next morning I got a phone call, so I went in and had an interview at Miege. I became the head football coach there in 2006. It was in December or January when I took the job, but shortly afterward I got a phone call from Carl. He said, "Do you have any interest in going and doing an internship with NFL Europe?"

That was just going to be in the winter—probably just in February and into March—and then I'd be done in Europe. When I got there, I started coaching the tackles and the tight ends. They needed an offensive line coach and they asked me if I had any interest in doing it. I agreed and had to call Bishop Miege and tell them I wouldn't be there until June. I was a little nervous about that, but they were okay with that. So Sarah and I and the kids went to Cologne, Germany. Sarah homeschooled the kids there for eight weeks while I was coaching. They traveled all over Europe while I went to the basement of a soccer stadium, so it wasn't the most exciting thing.

After that one season in Germany, I came back and coached at Bishop Miege until 2011. Then Charlie Weis called and asked if I wanted to be on his staff at KU. Charlie had offered me a job in 2010 at Notre Dame, but it just wasn't right. I kind of knew he wasn't going to be around there very long. I didn't want to take my family and move if I wasn't going to be around there for a while. But with the KU job, we could stay in our house in Kansas City, and I could commute. So I coached at KU for a couple of years. After a game against Texas, I was sitting in the locker room with Charlie. I said, "This just isn't for me. I appreciate you giving me the opportunity. I think I just started a little bit too late."

When you start coaching college football at 45 years old, you're just not used to the hours. You're not used to the recruiting. It was just too much. I just wasn't happy. Lou Holtz used to say all the time, "If you're not happy, you're not going to do your best."

I just wasn't happy. I stepped down from there and went back and coached at Miege as the offensive line coach. We won four straight state championships. Then, when Colin went to Notre Dame and was playing a little bit, I didn't want to miss those games. So for three years, I stopped coaching altogether and watched Colin play. I didn't want to be traveling back and forth and I wanted to give 100 percent to the program. Once Colin went to KU, I went back to Bishop Miege and I'm still there.

In the opening of my segments on Soren Petro's show on 810 WHB in Kansas City, the voice over says I "started out with football, then radio, then football, then radio again, then football." That's kind of the way it was. Those are the two passions I have right now: coaching and doing radio. They're both the same. It's about sharing the love of the game. The more people understand about this great game, the more they enjoy it, the more they want to watch it, the more intrigued they are, and the more fanatical they are.

I always thought that if you give kids an opportunity to play football, they'd love it. But I also want to give people the opportunity to understand the game so they can enjoy it more. When they're watching the game and they see something happen, they can say, "I thought that was going to happen," or "This is why it happened." They're never going to understand the game as much as the coach does, but if they can watch the game with a little bit more knowledge, it just makes it so much better.

I think Chiefs fans are among the most educated fans because we, as players and hosts of radio shows, have done a really nice job of explaining the game and explaining the back side of the game, which makes them love it even more. My radio career started right after I retired at the end of the 2000 season. We started *CrunchTime* with Frank Boal and Bill Maas. We were ranked in the top of our market for most of the quarters. It was a great show, and we enjoyed it. We had a lot of fun with it. There was a lot of slapstick humor, a lot of really digging deep into the game, explaining the game, and having people understand what was going on behind the scenes and on the field. That lasted for about three or four years.

One of the biggest mistakes I ever made was leaving 810 and going to 610, a new all-sports station owned by the people who owned 980. It's not that I hated the work or the people. I really liked the people there. I met a lot of good people. A lot of guys, who are over at 810 now, were there. But when I made that transition with Bill and Jason Whitlock, I never felt comfortable. I kind of got talked into going, so I left Frank and went over to 610. That partnership didn't last long, and I had several other partners on the air for a while. Then I had my own show for two years. I lacked a lot of support because I didn't really have a producer. In a way I kind of had to produce my own show, which was a lot of work.

I finally made the decision to go back to 810 and I've been there ever since. I'm a guest analyst on two of the daytime shows. I have a different role with each one. For *The Border Patrol,* they want someone to join in on their banter. With *The Program* Soren and I spend a majority of our time analyzing the games and the players. I also cohost *CrunchTime* with Frank on a weekly basis. That's my most rewarding radio hour because Frank and I have been working together since early in my playing career. We talk current events and the Chiefs. My favorite part is a segment called "the good, the bad, and the ugly" from each Chiefs game. I like all three roles. They each give me a chance to share my knowledge and love of football.

Getting back to coaching, I learned a lesson in the very first year of it. There is a different relationship between players and coaches as opposed to players and players. In my first year, the first five or six games, the offensive line was not playing very well. I wasn't coaching well because I was coaching as a player and a friend, not as a coach. They didn't respect me much. They respected me, but it was a different relationship that I needed to establish, and I realized that pretty quickly. Once we turned that around a little bit and reined that in, we just took off. They played really well and won the state championship. As a player who loved to be around the guys, loved the camaraderie, I always prided myself in being one of the guys. You can't do that as a coach, and I learned that my first year.

We hear all the time about the Xs and Os coaches as opposed to being a player's coach. Players like to play for a players' coach because he gets along with them better than an Xs and Os coach. But there's a difference between being a players' coach and being one of the guys. To be a players' coach, you're walking a fine line. You want to have open communication. You want to value their insight and their ideas. But you're in a different kind of relationship. Being a friend is okay, but when it comes to the nitty gritty of it, when you need to really clamp down on somebody, you've got to have that respect and discipline in order for them to listen. Some guys are good at it, and some guys aren't.

If you love the players and you care for them, you want to give them the best opportunity to have success. In high school you want to give them the best opportunity to have some confidence in their lives using football. I always tell kids, "If you want to play football in college, there is a program out there for you." There are all kinds of different levels and all kinds of different places. They may not be Alabama or Notre Dame, but there's Division II and Division III.

When you get to college, it's all about time management and discipline. You see a kid who goes to college and goes off track because he or she has so much free time and doesn't know how to budget the time correctly. It doesn't matter if the kid plays football, softball, or basketball, you have to have that discipline and that time management. There are times that you are practicing and times you are with your teammates. You have a responsibility to do the right thing because you don't want to affect your teammates negatively.

Coaching is really not about football. It's about preparing these kids for challenges, preparing them for life, preparing them to channel their energies successfully. It's about all those things. Football is merely the vehicle. I was always told that football is like a triangle. Everybody starts out in Pop Warner at the base of that triangle, and it's deep and wide. As you get to high school, it gets a little smaller. In college it gets smaller, and the very little tip at the top of the triangle is the professional athlete. In the middle of that is the game of football. It has lessons that can be learned—no matter what level you're at or how far you get.

I've coached at every level. I've coached in NFL Europe at the professional level. I've coached at the University of Kansas. I've been the head coach of a high school football team. I've been the assistant coach of a high school football team. All those roles are a little bit different, but there are challenges in each one of them. I often tell people that the most innocent, the most vulnerable, and the most important level is the high school level because you're teaching the basics. All those skillsets that they take for granted in college and in the pros have to be taught in high school in order for them to have success. It's those steps you need to have to have a winning program.

I recently did a pregame speech for a high school team. I told them I'd played at every level. I played in the NFL and ran out onto the field at Arrowhead Stadium in front of almost 80,000 screaming people. I played on the road in Oakland, where you took your life in your hands running out on the field. I played in The Big House at Michigan with 106,000 people. I played in one of the greatest college football games of all time between Miami and Notre Dame.

But I told them if I could pick one more game to play, I'd always pick one more high school game. Everybody was on the same page with just one goal: to bring pride to the school, and there was such camaraderie and love and the commitment of those kids. That to me is the best of football. Friday nights to me to this day give me more goosebumps than anything else would.

One of the other things that my platform of former professional football player gave me is to endorse products. I've done my share, but there are a few that stick out. I'll start with CBD American Shaman. It's easy to say that's it's a sponsorship deal. I'm getting paid to endorse the product, but this is something that is really important to me because it's helped me.

I was a born skeptic. You hear about different remedies or pain-relief products that people throw out there, but you're never quite sure if they're going to work. I was doing a radio segment away from the studio with Soren Petro at a CBD store. The first thing Soren told me was, "This isn't marijuana. Don't come in making jokes because they don't think it is funny."

I walked in, and Jamie Woolard, the CEO, was there. He said, "Are you sore anywhere? Do you have any problems? We'd love for you to try..."

I said, "Sore anywhere? I'm always sore. But my shoulder has been horrible lately."

He said, "Let me put some of this anti-inflammatory cream on it." He put some on it, and it kicked in pretty quickly. About halfway through the show, I started to feel better. I was sold at that point and I decided to give it try. I was going to get involved and introduce it to NFL alumni during the Hall of Fame proceedings. I made some presentations to some of the alumni boards. The NFL is still kind of leery of some of the CBD products. I think they're coming around, but they're still a little hesitant.

I've turned so many people on to the anti-inflammatory and the water solubles for circulation, anxiety, and pain relief, especially some of the former players. It really has been a blessing not just for me, but also for players who didn't have another option other than opioids. The opioid crisis is so bad right now in the NFL. In my little world in the NFL, I have many friends and people I've played against who have become addicted to opioids. If you can give somebody else an option that is all natural and can help, it makes you feel good in more than one way.

Really what it came down to with me was looking for something after Mike Webster's untimely passing. I always felt like I could have done more for him. He was there at the lowest point in my life. He was able to kind of kickstart me and give me an opportunity to have a career in the NFL. I wasn't there for him. Fast forward to this opportunity. If I could help somebody not fall into the perils of opioids or not fall into the perils of prescription drugs like Webby did, then maybe that could ease my soul a little bit. CBD American Shaman gave me that opportunity. I am forever grateful.

It's great to have some outside income and it's great to be involved with a Kansas City company that is a really good, up-and-coming company with many, many stores around the metro. More importantly, it gives me an opportunity to share a choice with people who have pain. I always say, "Pain sucks. If you can do anything to counteract that pain, you do it."

When I first started using this product, I was rubbing it on my shoulder and on my knees. I had eight or nine surgeries on my left knee. I've had a couple of surgeries on my right knee and on my elbow. I ended up having knee replacements. My hands were also very arthritic. When you're a center, your hands are always going to be beat up. I remember Webster's hands. I would see all his knuckles that were out of joint and crooked. He would always be talking about how sore his hands were and how numb his hands were. The circulation was bad. The one thing I dreaded was shaking a person's hand if they squeezed it too hard. I always had pain in my hand with golf and doing a little work around the house. But after a few weeks of rubbing the cream on my knees and shoulders, I noticed that my hands were feeling great. It did more work on my hands than anything else.

I also sleep better. I wake up in the morning, and the circulation is better and I can get into my day better. I have been able to share it with guys on the golf course who never played a sport in their lives, but their backs are sore and hurting. It just makes me feel good to make other people's pain go away because pain sucks.

One of the things that I had to learn was to fill the void of the adrenaline rush of the NFL. The pain we were just discussing is masked by that weekly rush. Once your career ends, the rush ends with it, but the pain continues. The need for the rush and not just to mask the pain is very real. If you're not prepared for the next step, you can be in big trouble.

The crazy thing about playing sports is that there is a lot of life after you're done. If you're a businessman, you're right in the midst of everything until you're well into your 60s most of the time. But in the life of the professional athlete, especially in the NFL, you're basically done by 30. I was fortunate in that I played until I was 32. There is a lot of life after that.

Initially, I made some poor choices about ways to fill that void of the NFL through drinking and different issues like that. I've tried to share with people that you can fall into that trap. Nobody asked me if I wanted to continue to play football. My body basically told me I couldn't play football anymore. Just like Lou used to say to us all the time, "If you don't practice one day in the week, you know it. If you don't practice two days during the week, your coach knows it. If you don't practice three days and you go play, everybody knows it."

The key for me was to get out when I knew it and not when the coach and everybody else knew it. I was able to do that, but it felt like it was a death. I was looking for something, and that's why I got into the radio and coaching just to fill that void. So many guys have financial and emotional difficulties after the NFL. That transition is very tough. I don't care if you have a great support unit. My wife has been my best friend since we were 18 years old. We met at Notre Dame when we were freshmen. I had a best friend first and a wife second. Thank God that I did because if I didn't, I would just have fallen into that same pattern that a lot of guys have fallen into.

There are a lot of divorces, a lot of people lose their families once they get out of the NFL. It's such a destructive spiral. Some people make it out, and some people don't. I've tried to share with people that there are other things to fill that void, even though it doesn't feel like it at the time you retire. The brain is so trained to crave that adrenaline, emotion, and excitement that when it's taken away, you want to fill it with other things, whether it is drugs, alcohol, or illicit behavior. Everybody has to face that demon at some point. Nobody gets out without some kind of mental or physical wound. You have to be able to face it.

It's similar to the practice idea. If you don't deal with it for one day, you'll know it. If you don't deal with it for two days, your spouse, your kids, or your close friends will know it. If you don't deal with it for three days, everybody will know it because you'll be off the deep end, or you will be found in places you shouldn't be. Just like practice, it is a daily thing that you have to address head on.

Football is a microcosm of life. You're going to have fourth-down situations. You've got to learn to convert. You can't punt. Sometimes you've got to go for it. You've got to go on. You've got to keep that drive going. You'll fall on your ass sometimes, but if you don't deal with it every day, if you're not focused on your mental and physical well-being, it won't be long before the wheels fall off. There are options—whether that is going and speaking with professionals or finding a support group through the NFL alumni. Maybe it's pouring into your spouse and your family. Maybe it's working out and taking care of your body.

Football is all or nothing, and that is a problem. You see guys after they retire who balloon up to 400 pounds. You see other guys who look like they could still play because they are in such great shape. You see guys that make that adjustment and really do great things and really try to help other people and you see people who just fade away. You have suicides and you have guys you never hear from again. They just disappear. That is the nature of this crazy sport because you have to be all in.

It was probably a little easier for me. Because as an offensive lineman, people weren't chanting my name nearly as often as they were for Joe Montana or Marcus Allen. But you've got to find your sweet spot of routines. You've got to find your daily affirmations. You've got to find those things that keep you happy, that keep you focused, that keep you whole. Most of the time, 25 to 30 years out, you either find that sweet spot, knowing where you need to be and how you need to do things or you're looking for answers in the wrong spots. It's a natural thing. You're looking for that quick fix. You're looking for something that will take that mental, physical pain, and sometimes you get lost.

One of the things that was important for me is that I had a support group, and that was the Chiefs fans. I tried to find ways to stay relevant, to stay part of the fabric of this community—whether it was through charitable work, through radio shows, through coaching kids, through being involved in the school community, or through going out and speaking to different groups. That was more for me than it was for them. People would say that it's so great that you coach those kids. But I knew myself. I knew that my support group was the Kansas City fan from the very first minute that I came into Kansas City to the minute that I retired from the field.

That's why I was so emotional on the night of November 1, when I got inducted into the Chiefs Hall of Fame. I spent my professional career giving my best to the Chiefs fans. That night I was surrounded by so many of them who let me know they appreciated it. The Chiefs did a little ceremony for me on the field before my last game. I knew that my support group was those people who were there on Sundays. I get along well with them now. It's like a family. You may have people in your family that you may not particularly like, but they're your family. This is not trying to appease anybody, but I'm just telling you that I needed the Chiefs fans and the people here in Kansas City as much as I needed any other kind of therapy. That's why I stayed involved in this community. I was afraid that if I had gone to Phoenix, Arizona, or had gone back to Chicago or to New Jersey, where Sarah grew up, I would have lost that.

I trusted those people. You can't heal unless you trust. I trusted the Chiefs fans. Even though we don't all get along, I still know that they're there for me. That's a big group of people. But there is a group of people who went to my radio shows that started in 1992. They went to just about every one of my appearances on the road. That group of people has always been there, and they are really important to me as a support group. As far as any particular fans, I don't want to mention names because I'll leave out somebody. But it's really that group of people that embraced me back in the early '90s. They connected with me, and I connected with them. They supported everything.

When you have people lining up to get into a radio show or people lining up at the airport after a game—win, lose, or any time you do anything—you can't help but become attached to them. I always say that if you ask Kansas City to help you with a particular cause, a particular charitable work, or anything like that, they're always there for you. The Chiefs fanbase has always been there for me.

Of course, there are people I do want to mention specifically. When I first came into the league, I had an agent named Steve Zucker. He was out of Chicago. I also interviewed with former Chiefs lineman Tom Condon as well. When Tom came to Chicago to talk with my family, my dad and I picked him up in an old 1979 GM pickup truck. It was a bench seat. Tom came to the door, I got out, and he slid in, and he had to sit there between my dad and me.

Here was this Chicago cop who probably had his pistol sitting right there next to him. Tom was sitting there with his legs crossed and his hands crossed in between these two big behemoths from the south side of Chicago. He told me later that he had never been intimidated by any defensive lineman more than he had been sitting between the two of us.

We developed a really good relationship, and I really liked Tom. I really wanted to go with Tom, but my dad said, "I know where Steve Zucker's office is located. He's in Chicago. If he ever screws you around, I'll go find him." How do you argue with that?

After I was drafted by the Chiefs, I let Zucker go, and Tom did the next part of my contract pro bono because I was still paying Zucker the first four years. Then Tom negotiated the next two contracts for me. Tom and Ken Kremer were two great guys. Ken picked me up, and we went around looking for a wedding ring for my wife. Those guys were my support base and they were my friends and the people I relied on.

Tom stepped up for me one time when I didn't really want him to, but he was right. It was probably about 1992 or 1993, right before Montana got here. I just felt like we weren't going anywhere as a team. I called Tom and said I wanted to be traded to the Chicago Bears. I said, "I have my friends and my family there. That's where I want to go."

He said, "Okay, I'll call you back."

The rest of the day he never called me back. The next day I said, "I never heard from you."

He said, "Listen, dumbass, I knew you were just being emotional. I knew you were making poor decisions. I never called the Chiefs."

I said, "Thank you."

I was lucky to have someone I could trust, a person who knew me, a person who knew the best thing for me. I probably could have made more money with a trade and renegotiations and all those things. That's not the way Tom was. Tom knew the best thing for me was to be here in Kansas City, to be here with this team and this city, so he talked me off the cliff.

People often have the wrong idea about agents. The impression is they're sitting in their three-piece suits in their offices, and all they do is negotiate your contracts. They do far more than that. They're your confidants and your friends who basically have your financial best interest and your personal best interest at heart, maybe even at their own expense. The biggest and most important decision someone will make in their NFL career is who they'll hire to be their representative. Some guys hire people because they're flashy, or maybe somebody else had a good experience with them. But they've got to have your back. There has to be that personal connection that goes far beyond the contract negotiation. I've seen people get themselves in financial issues. I've seen people get themselves into issues with their organization and everything else just because of hiring the wrong person to represent them.

The other thing you have to learn when you hire an agent is that they work for you. You don't work for them. It's hard for a 22- or 23-year-old kid to recognize that the guy you just hired is working for you. But you have to hire somebody who has a backbone and a conscience and somebody who can stand up to you if you're making a bad decision. You don't want a yes man.

That's what Tom and Ken were for me. They were there for me. They were my friends and they had my best interest. They didn't let me screw up when there were many opportunities where I probably could have done so.

After games Tom and Ken would be down in the tunnel. They would have clients from other teams, but they would be down there to chat with me. The first guys I would always go to would be those guys. I'd ask, "What do you think? How did I play?" They would be honest. They would tell me I played well or struggled on something. Both of them had been offensive linemen, and I knew that they were going to tell me the truth. It was really a good thing for me. It kept me grounded. It kept me focused. It kept me aware.

If you hire somebody who is just going to say that everything is great, the next thing you know, you're getting cut or getting a crappy contract. The next thing you know, you've lost a lot of money in bad investments because they're really looking out for themselves and telling you what you want to hear. I can't tell you how many guys I've seen through the years of playing and coaching that make bad decisions but just won't listen. It's that weird dynamic that for some guys it just doesn't work out. You hope the best for them, but some of the time, it just doesn't work out.

I also want to talk about my relationship with the media. So many athletes say they don't have time to talk to the media. If it were not for the media, they'd have to have an offseason job. They'd be playing the game for a small percentage of the gate. But because of the media, they're making millions of dollars. The ones who really irritate the members of the media are the ones who were like that in their playing careers and then become part of the media and change completely. I tried not to be like that. I wanted to be approachable not only because I wanted publicity for my charity, but also because I respected them.

My dad used to say all the time, "You're a cockroach or an ant." A cockroach is great when the lights are off in the room. When the lights go on, they scatter. When things get tough, they hide. They go into the crawl space and they're gone. When you turn the lights on and put the focus on the ants, they stay in line. They stay focused on their task. They're proud of who they are and what they have to do. I always wanted to be an ant. There are so many players who are cockroaches.

I'm not trying to be dismissive of anybody, but when you're winning, everybody stays around the locker room. They're there for everybody. When they lose, they're taking off as fast as they can. They don't like the lights on them when they're losing. If you choose to be an ant, be there for the good or the bad. The light's on if you're doing well, the light's on you if you lose, and you've still got to be there.

Maybe because I did radio early in my career, I realized that the media had a job to do. Did I get along with every journalist? No, but I always tried to respect them. There's a great parable: you can attract more flies with honey than with vinegar. If you're in there and you're spewing vinegar, then the media is going to treat you negatively. But if you're there answering questions and being honest and truthful, they'll be respectful of you. I always took it as a challenge to communicate and stand in front of the cameras when we lost, when everybody else was trying to dodge out of the way.

Frank Boal has really been a father to me since my dad passed away. We've done radio shows together. Frank has always treated me very well. Other people in the media would get upset with Frank because he would come up to me and talk, and I'd always be there for Frank. You know how it is in the media. When one person talks, then all of a sudden 20 other people come piling on in. I would always say "Frank" when I was answering his question, so he could use the soundbite but nobody else could.

I had a personal relationship with guys like Todd Leabo, Soren, Don Fortune, Al Wallace, and the cameramen who were with them. They always covered me fairly because I was always there taking the fire when nobody else would. I learned just to be a man about wins and losses. You're going to win some and you're going to lose some. I always took it as a challenge to stay in there and be proud and give people forthright answers. Yeah, you've got to have a little bit of prepared speech, a little bit of coach speak, but you can do that in a way to help them if they're doing their job, and they get what they need out of it. Naturally, when you need something from them, they'll be there for you. I always thought we had a pretty good relationship.

Speaking of strong relationships, I, of course, want to mention my family. Even though my wife is from New Jersey, she likes it in Kansas City. My kids have only known Kansas City. They were the reason I didn't sign with another team at the end of my Chiefs career. I knew I couldn't leave Kansas City. I knew I had to be present in the lives of my kids.

When I had a chance to coach at Notre Dame, Lou Holtz said, "Don't mess with happy."

I did that one time. I messed with happy when I went to coach at Kansas, even though we didn't have to move. I wanted to coach college football. I thought I could do it. I loved coaching at the University of Kansas. I loved being around college kids, but I also felt like I was living the song, "Cat's in the Cradle." You remember the lyrics: "When you coming home, Dad? I don't know when, but we'll get together then."

My dad used to hate that song. When that song came on, he would turn it off. He felt like he worked so much and wasn't there enough for us. I always said I'd never be that guy. Well, I was mostly gone for two years at a really important time for my kids. It just wasn't the right decision, and I messed with happy. Even though my kids didn't have to move, I wasn't home. I wasn't around.

When you talk about our family, our rock always has been my wife. If it wasn't for her, I don't know where I would be. We started dating and we were best friends from 18 years old during the first semester of our freshman year. I met her at a party. We were playing Penn State that week, and Penn State was ranked No. 1.

She said, "Penn State is going to kill you guys."

I said, "I'll bet you dinner that we beat Penn State."

I knew either way I was going to win because we were either going to beat the No. 1 team or I would get a date with this gorgeous girl at Notre Dame. I didn't have anything to do with the outcome of the game—we lost 24–19—because I only played as a long snapper. But I won because there was no way she was going to buy me dinner. I don't know how I got the guts enough to go up and talk to her, but I did. I didn't have a car, so I borrowed a car from our kicker, John Carney. When I picked her up, it was snowing really hard. We went out to dinner at the local restaurant and we drove back to campus and had a campus snowball fight. And the rest is history.

I often tell people that we were friends first, and that's why we survived through the rough patches with bad decision making and other things. I survived because of Sarah, who is my best friend first. Sarah's always been there. She doesn't like the spotlight. She doesn't like to be out in front. She's not going to be one of those people who is going to go to the NFL wives' luncheon and make a speech. She is the support system for our family. She is the rock. When you've got a guy with a big mouth, a big personality like me, somebody's got to be the counterweight to that.

She's a great mother. Our kids are so well-adjusted and have done so well in school. It's just like anything else in life. If you have consistency in your life, you're going to have a better chance no matter what you're trying to do. Sarah has always been consistent, always been a loving, consistent person. Our kids have thrived because of her consistency. When I do all these things and I have the success that I have had, I always knew who I owed it to, and that's my wife.

It hasn't been easy to be my kids. That's one thing that has been hard for me. They would never admit it, but I know there has been undue pressure and undue spotlight put on them because of me. Some of them have thrived because of it, and some have pulled back because of it. I'll never forget: there was a nun at St. Ann's Church. She would say to my kids, "How come you never talk about your dad being a professional football player? He's a famous Chief."

They would say, "It just never comes up." It just wasn't what we did.

My daughter, Cailey, was an elite swimmer. She swam at the Olympic Trials. She was a Division I swimmer on scholarship at Notre Dame. She got up on the blocks one time, and one of the judges said, "Aren't you Tim Grunhard's daughter?" right before she swam! She said it kind of freaked her out.

One of the reasons I left the head coaching position at Bishop Miege was that my oldest, CJ, did not adjust well. He was a freshman at Miege when I was the head coach. It just wasn't working. He was pulling back. I don't think he was as healthy socially because of that. I told Sarah, "If I go, he'll be on his own and he'll be able to grow," and he did.

Colin was the opposite. He didn't give a crap. He was fine being Tim Grunhard's son, but CJ had issues with it. My kids are all very good academically and athletically. More importantly, they're just good, solid citizens, and that's really because of my wife and her consistency. I'm so proud of what they've become. CJ is a commodities trader. Cailey works for a digital design company in Cincinnati, Ohio. Colin is getting his MBA and playing football at Kansas. Cassie, my youngest, is in her senior year of nursing school. She's just really taken to nursing.

My kids are happy and doing well. Once again it kind of goes back to what Holtz said: "Don't mess with happy." If you find something that makes you happy, if you find something that is fulfilling for you, if you find something that makes you whole as a person, don't mess with it. Thanks, Chiefs Kingdom, for helping me find what makes me happy.

Acknowledgments

YOU MIGHT LOOK AT ME AS A MEMBER OF THE CHIEFS RING OF Honor and Hall of Fame. That may be true, but it wouldn't be true if not for a lot of people. I want to take this time to thank them for investing in me and in this project.

First, I want to thank the Hunt family, beginning with Lamar and Norma, for bringing this great organization to Kansas City and giving me an opportunity to find a new home and to be a part of your extended family. I want to thank Clark Hunt for continuing the great tradition of love, trust, and commitment that the Hunts have for the Kansas City Chiefs organization. Clark has carried that on and brought it into the 21st century. He has kept that feeling of family—even in this day and age where the NFL is so corporate. I'm no longer an active player, but as a fan, I thank you for giving us an organization and a team we can be proud of.

I want to thank Carl Peterson and Marty Schottenheimer for believing in a 21 year old from Chicago who they drafted in the second round with the 40th pick. They saw something in me that I didn't know I had and they challenged me to become one of the better players in the Chiefs organization. Their foresight and their belief are what drove me to become part of the Hall of Fame in Kansas City. I also want to thank my offensive line coaches, starting with Howard Mudd to Alex Gibbs to Art Shell and Mike Solari. All of them brought different techniques and fundamentals and different ways to share their love for the game.

I want to thank my teammates. There are so many that I really don't want to name anyone in particular. They are my family. As I say in this book, a lot of times you can't do this thing called football for yourself. The hurt and the pain, the suffering, and the toughness that it takes is impossible unless you're doing it for somebody else. I always did it for my teammates. We've gone through a lot of battles, a lot of blood, sweat, and tears to become close. They taught me to respect people of all different backgrounds.

Next, I want to thank Amanda Carlo, the Chiefs' community and alumni relations manager, for being in my corner and being my support system in my post-playing career with the Chiefs. She's been a constant supporter, encouraging me to get outside my comfort zone as far as promoting myself.

I want to thank the Kansas City fans because their enthusiasm and dedication to the Chiefs is what drove me to play with the intensity and the enthusiasm and the toughness that I needed. I always wanted to be a direct reflection of the Kansas City Chiefs fans.

I want to thank the people at Triumph Books for making this process very easy. They gave me great guidance and direction as I tried to put together a book honoring the decade of the '90s, not only for the Kansas City Chiefs players, but also the Kansas City Chiefs fans.

I want to thank my coauthor, David Smale. Thank you for making this process go smoothly. I enjoyed every minute of our conversations. Your expertise in this whole process helped me resurrect some great memories that really made me fall in love with the Chiefs again in a different way.

I want to thank my parents. My father always challenged me to get out of my comfort zone and strive to become a man. My mother was a supportive and loving partner in my life. She was always there through thick and thin.

I want to thank my kids, CJ, Colin, Cailey, and Cassie. They have always shown me and helped me experience what true love is all about.

I've saved the best for last. I want to thank my wife, Sarah. She is the most important person in my life. She has been in every project and everything I have done from the time we were 18 years old. She's been the wind beneath my wings. She's always kind of been in the background, yet been the force of motivation for me. She's always been on my side. I wouldn't be who I am without her.